The Interplay of East and West

Books by Barbara Ward

THE WEST AT BAY

POLICY FOR THE WEST

FAITH AND FREEDOM

THE INTERPLAY OF EAST AND WEST

FIVE IDEAS THAT CHANGE THE WORLD

INDIA AND THE WEST

THE RICH NATIONS AND THE POOR NATIONS

BARBARA WARD

THE INTERPLAY OF
East and West

Points of Conflict and Co-operation

With a New Epilogue

THE SIR EDWARD BEATTY
MEMORIAL LECTURES

The Norton Library
W · W · NORTON & COMPANY · INC ·
NEW YORK

Preface

THE SIR EDWARD BEATTY
MEMORIAL LECTURES, endowed by Miss Mary Beatty
and the late Dr. H. A. Beatty, are given annually as a
memorial to their brother, who for almost a quarter of
a century, until his death in 1943, served McGill University as its Chancellor. His contribution to the development of McGill was outstanding, and none who knew
him are ever likely to forget his vision and determination. He was among the truly great Canadians and these
lectures annually recall to generations of students who
could not know him personally the memory of his greatness.

Lady Jackson, more widely known to the world under
her maiden name as Barbara Ward, delivered the second series of Beatty Lectures in the autumn of 1955.
She took the same problem, so vitally important to our
generation, that Dr. Sarvepalli Radhakrishnan had discussed a year earlier—the relationship of East and West
—but has approached it from a different facet. The best
indication of the interest that her lectures evoked is the
simple statement that more than 2500 people—students,

professors, and other citizens of Montreal—turned up on three evenings in singularly wintry weather and sat silently attentive on the hard temporary seats that had been installed in The Sir Arthur Currie Memorial Gymnasium Armoury because none of the lecture halls in the University was large enough to hold the audience. The ovation that she received was sincere and heart-warming.

F. Cyril James
Principal and Vice-Chancellor
McGill University.

The Interplay of East and West

PART

1

B

EFORE we look at the contrasts and possibilities of co-operation between East and West, we have to remember one thing. This is the first time in the history of man that the working out of a relationship between the great civilizations of the Orient and ourselves is a matter of extreme urgency. We have lived in a world in the past where for long periods civilizations seemed as remote from each other as the planets do now. Whether, of course, the planets are going to remain remote is another interesting subject for inquiry, but, up to the very threshold of our own day,

(11)

it was perfectly possible for the Western world to conceive of itself in isolation as the center of all civilized living, and indeed, of all human experience and human experiment. Our new situation, in which we are jostled together with people of very different cultures, traditions, and backgrounds, is new, and one in which we are still feeling our way for the proper tools and instruments of conciliation and working together. Yet cooperation is virtually impossible without some meeting of minds. Therefore, we have to look at the past in order to understand the kind of preconceived ideas which are being brought to play on both sides in this new contact between East and West.

Maybe we think we understand our own ideas—and possibly we do—but we have also to fathom what other countries and other civilizations think about when they look at us. And here, a much greater effort of understanding is needed. Yet this lack of understanding of other peoples' view of the West is a particularly important point to remember because, in the last four or five hundred years, the Western world has been the aggressive, outgoing, and indeed, disturbing force for all other civilizations and ways of life. We tend to concentrate today on the Communists' pressure upon the frontiers of our Western world but, in point of fact, this pressure on us is new. For the last four hundred years it is we of the West who have been doing the pressing, it is we who have been stirring the world up with the vigor and—all too often—the blind drive of our own dynamic development, of our own self-assurance, of our own ideas.

This outward drive of Western civilization, which was, until yesterday, the dominant feature in world history, is not always understood by us. So if we are to find ways and means of living peacefully, East and West, in our narrow world together, it is essential for us to have an idea of how we, the Westerners, have been behaving recently, how our history looks to others, and the kind of contacts with other peoples we have enjoyed or imposed or suffered in the past.

Let us go back, then, about two or three thousand years. After all, two or three thousand years is a very short time in the history of mankind. We may tend to think of it as a long, long span, but this is not so. Mankind as a going concern, as a recognizably human community, has been operating now for about a hundred thousand years. Our experiments in advanced civilization, which go back no more than four or five thousand years, are relatively brief. Today, indeed, we may well be occupied in making them briefer still, but on any time scale, the few thousand years of developed civilization fills a relatively short span either in human development or in the infinitely longer evolution of life itself.

The point of time at which the civilizations of the world began to have contact with each other seems to have lain between a thousand and five hundred B.C. Until that millennium, one could hardly call the relations between various parts of the earth's surface as "contacts between civilizations," because civilization, as a recognizable form of human social endeavor, was still circumscribed in time and place. Before that epoch, the great centers of nascent civilization—the Yellow River basin in China, the North Indian river system, the irrigated areas of the Middle East—had been established and cultural, social, and political influences began to radiate outward from them. Civilizations of a persistent and recognizable kind grew and spread—in spite of vicissitudes of conquest and internal crisis—in China, India, Mesopotamia, and Egypt. And in the fifteen hundred years before the birth of Christ, contact was established between them and the peoples we in the West number among our own cultural forebears—the restless, dynamic peoples of the Mediterranean who, at that time, were coming more and more under the influence of Greek thought and enterprise.

There followed about a thousand years of contact and exchange. If one might summarize in a gross simplification this millennium of fluctuating but often intensive contact, one could say that between India and China and the West, exchanges were in the main commercial and involved little social or political influence. In the first century A.D. Roman ships found their way, by the monsoon routes, to India and later to China and for the first time an organized Western society acquired an appetite for the products and luxuries of the Orient. Chinese silk, for instance, came to play an important part in what we should now call the problem of Rome's balance of payments. As taste for this article spread from the very rich to wider classes, writers were found denouncing forms of consumption which undermined the Empire's economy—a complaint one seems to have heard on later occasions and a reminder of how very old some of our newest problems may be.

Later, when the Western capital had moved from Rome to Byzantium and the Arabs had taken over the Southern trade routes to India, commerce continued with the northern caravans and the Tang regime in China had contact with the Byzantine emperors—to whose frontiers a temporary expansion of Chinese power westwards almost reached. But nomad incursions from the steppes endangered these lines of communication and they and China together were swallowed up in the Mongol invasion.

In the Middle East, in the quadrilateral bounded on the West and East by the Eastern Mediterranean and the coasts of India and on the North and South by the Caspian Sea and the Arabian deserts, the meeting of civilizations was direct and violent. One remembers Xerxes bringing Indian contingents in his mighty imperial army to attack Greece and Alexander's Macedonians advancing, in return, to the great rivers of Northern India and leaving behind them, for centuries, a Hellenized order of society stretching from the Aegean to the frontiers of India. Then this same area, first with the incursion of the Arabs from the South and later of the Mongols from the North became a barrier between the West and India and China which was decisively broken only when, at the end of the fifteenth century, the Portuguese opened the sea route to India round the Cape.*

Now, I believe that one can discover a clue to the relationships between East and West by attempting to compare the kind of contact which occurred before this long historical interregnum with the kind of contact which emerged at what we might call the beginning of the modern era—shall we say, the beginning of the six-

* I do not mean to suggest that the Arab-Moslem civilization which spread over North Africa and the Middle East was a negative force, comparable to the incursions of Northern nomads such as the Mongols, who evolved no native culture and left little mark on the great shores of history once their tide receded. For centuries, brilliant centers of Arab learning and civilization from Cordoba to Baghdad enjoyed an infinitely higher level of living than the barbarian heirs of Rome in Europe whom the Arabs in fact despised as clumsy and oafish. "Their bellies are big, their colour pale, their hair long and lank. They lack keenness of understanding and clarity of intelligence." Such was the verdict of an eleventh-century Moslem of Toledo. The point here is that the Arabs and later the Mongols effectively cut Europe off for centuries from any direct knowledge of the East.

teenth century. During that time, broadly speaking, the great Oriental civilizations, in spite of superficial changes —rise and fall of dynasties, frontier clashes, Mongol pressure—remained virtually unchanged in all their basic social and economic institutions and in their outlook and philosophy. What happened in Europe, on the contrary, was something almost as new and explosive as the discovery of the atom. In the first phase of contact, one can risk the generalization that like was coming into touch with like. After the fifteenth century, this was no longer true. Asia might not have changed. But Europe was attempting "to make all things new."

Now let us look at the ancient societies at the time of the earlier contacts. To do so, we must attempt some schematic divisions. In history and, indeed, in other forms of knowledge, such divisions tend to be arbitrary compartments, adopted for convenience's sake, and they can destroy balance and disrupt the organic unity of the subject. But our theme is so large that there must be some dividing up. So we will take the contact between East and West on three levels. One is the ideological plane or, if you like, the whole area of religion and philosophy. The next is the political level, the types of organization and government. The third is the economic system, the material substructure of society.

After 500 B.C., in the millennium during which contact between East and West was relatively continuous, their great civilizations on the whole resembled each other more than they differed. In the first place, by 500 B.C. all had reached a similar and decisive stage in the history of human thought. In China, in India, and in the Mediterranean world, in other words, in three contemporary centers of advanced civilization, there had occurred the same kind of reaching out—philosophically and religiously—to new concepts of the Godhead, of the relations between God and man, and hence of the whole organization of society. Before this revolutionary change, man had known two fundamental approaches to religion, which were closely allied. One was primitive and tribal—animism, the belief that all natural forces were in some way an expression of divine power, and the worship of the power itself, under the various natural forms in which it presented itself—earth, sea, sky, mountain, the local harvest crops. This "animation" of all natural surroundings with more than human power, mysterious, magical, and therefore religious, was man's first reaction to the "why" and the "how" of the universe, and he lived with it for a hundred thousand years. Indeed, in parts of the world today, for example in parts of West Africa, he still lives more or less under the same dispensation—uneasily seeking to combine it with modern forms of thought.°

° I cannot resist quoting one example from West Africa of the complexity of this mixture. If plans drawn up for a new dam and its reservoir involve the flooding-over of the sites of local fetishes,

With the development of settled agriculture and mankind's growing familiarity with the cycle of the farmer's year, what one might call a more sophisticated animism arose based upon the fertility of the soil and the rhythm of agriculture. The forces of nature were still worshiped but not so much in the small godlings of field and tree and mountain but in the great deities of the agricultural cycle, above all, in the Goddess of Fertility.

These systems—whether of primitive animism or the archaic fertility religion—were essentially polytheistic. Men worshiped many gods, small and great. And they were essentially fatalistic, leaving man bound to the great recurrences of nature. But at the period of history when contact between civilizations was about to begin, there had occurred in India, then China, and then the Mediterranean—largely under the leadership of men of great insight and extreme holiness of character—a reaching out toward new concepts.

In place of many gods, there was a single Godhead, source of being, or foundation of moral order. In place of the old rituals and propitiations, which remained external to man, came the idea of a religion of the spirit which man must practice in his heart, thus fulfilling the will of God, the divine order, in creation. And in place

---

then a calculation has to be made of the income necessary to propitiate and compensate the fetish priests and this income must be covered in the final cost of electricity.

of a humanity accepting blindly its place in a material, fertile, and mysterious universe, there began to emerge the figure of man raised above the material order by his sharing, at the base of his soul, in the Divine Being and by his capacity to choose or reject the law of God which would give life more abundantly. In varying measure and with diverse emphasis, these three concepts were the basis of the spiritual revolution wrought by such men as the writers of the Hindu Vedas, by Buddha and Confucius in Asia, by Greek philosophers and Jewish prophets in the West. Probably, when our whole story is told, if it ever is told, this spiritual change will be regarded as a revolution in mankind far greater than any of the material revolutions that have since occurred.

Now, at the time when contacts between civilizations began, comparable insights had appeared in all the great societies and it is hard for us to say whether, for example, Indian philosophy at that time influenced Greek philosophy or vice versa, for much of the contact was between people who had a similar approach and who were making a similar search. And yet we can observe small warning lights flashing on, as it were, to suggest that the later development of the Western world would not follow the same pattern as that of other civilizations.

In spite of the spiritual revolution in Hindu, Buddhist, and Confucian thought, one archaic concept retained its influence—the idea of a material reality bound to a recurring wheel of change. For Indian thought, this reality was illusion and one escaped from it into the limitless ocean of Being. In China, the material order was the real substance of man's life and could be restored to harmony by obedience to the moral law. It would then revolve in orderly fashion, unchanged in the perfect pattern established millennia before by the Yellow Emperor. Both attitudes limited the range of man's thinking about material reality—the Hindus by rejecting its importance, the Chinese by innate conservatism.

But in the West, the Jews and the Greeks were beginning to display a different attitude to the universe. The Jews had the idea that man could find the purpose of the Godhead in time and in history. They did not regard the whole pageant of material things as being largely meaningless, or as already fixed by a standard perfection achieved in the past. They believed in a progressive unfolding of God's purpose in time. They believed they, as a Chosen People, were actors in this drama. It was a role they might accept or reject. They were active participants in history and history had a meaning. Although such ideas may seem remote from our contemporary outlook, in them lay the seed of personal freedom, belief in progress, concern with material things—all of which are dominant ideas in the development of Western civilization.

Greek philosophy likewise gave evidence of a new

turn of thought. There is a story that Indian philosophers came to Greece and discussed philosophy with Socrates. They pressed him to tell them with what was Greek philosophy concerned. Socrates is reputed to have answered: Why, it is concerned with the study of all things human. At which point the Indian philosophers laughed and said: How can you study anything human until you know what is Divine? This anecdote gives a hint of the later divergence. The Greeks possessed an overwhelming curiosity about all things human, a belief, expressed most fully in the philosophy of Aristotle, that man could find in natural circumstances and in the structure of the world, matters of overwhelming interest in their own right and evidence, at the same time, of a divine order and harmony. Reason was the tool of this searching curiosity and its end the demonstration of an orderly universe. Intellectual search and scientific achievement—two hallmarks of the West—are implicit in the Greek approach.

Yet in general, the philosophy of the West, like that of the East, was still of a civilization emerging from the worship of a variety of gods, and from a fatalistic and recurrent concept of the universe to the notion of the single God (or Divine Law) and of a moral order for men reflecting the Divine.

Now, if we pass on to the field of government, the impression of like in contact with like is very strong. During the period of principal contact between the West and India and China, first Alexander, then the Roman Emperors, and at last the rulers of Byzantium did not display any really fundamental political differences from the governors of Eastern lands. The experiment of the free Greek city state had been extinguished before Alexander carried his conquests to India. The Hellenized order he left behind was despotic. The later empires all had common features—a large bureaucratic government by an imperial civil service drawing its authority solely from the explicitly divine or semidivine person of the Emperor. Whether it was Hadrian in the West, or the Mauryan Emperors in India, or the Han dynasty in China, this basic resemblance was more remarkable than any local variety in the political organization of the state.

Yet in the Western world there were signs of future difference. The Greek city states had been a unique experiment. In trading communities all along the Mediterranean they marked the emergence of the merchant class as an effective political force, and the first steps towards legal, constitutional, and representative government.

This point brings us to the economic substratum of politics. It is sometimes argued that the Greek experiment in free government can be explained primarily in terms of the growing commercial activity of the Greek city states while the static political farms of Asia were based on the empire's unchanging dependence upon agriculture, the peasantry, and the land tax. Certainly, this is one factor. In part by geographical accident, Europe was compelled to seek trade. Lying roughly between 55° and 35° north latitude, the continent had a narrow range of resources and lacked all tropical products. India and China, on the contrary, covered all types of climate and cultivation, and trade remained a marginal activity.

Yet there are reasons for doubting whether this important difference between East and West is decisive. The Phoenicians were keen traders—like the Greeks— but the Phoenician experiment in trading and colonizing ended in the despotic system of Carthage. Trade and the defense of trade routes were vital to Rome as they had been to Athens but the Roman Empire was consolidated on an imperial, autocratic pattern. Nor did a later trading people of the Eastern Mediterranean—the Arabs— break with autocracy. The contrast between a relatively immobile economy in the East and a more varied and commercial system in the West is an important one, but not decisive in the political sphere. Nor in the later days of the Roman Empire and during the period of Byzantium was it so important economically. By that time, in the West as in the East, land and the land tax and the exploitation of estates were the preponderant sources of wealth.

So in this first millennium of contact between East and West, you could not say that the civilizations were so divergent that the result of contact between them would be collision or conflict, or even a very fruitful exchange of ideas. To this there is the one exception—the Greek incursion into the Middle East, which had repercussions further afield in India and China where Hellenistic influence can be seen in the religious art of Mahayanan Buddhism. But it cannot be said that Greek influence profoundly changed either philosophy, government, or economic organization even in Syria or Persia. In short, contacts were not very profound and the chief element lay in the exchange of goods.

Now we pass on through five or six hundred years of history during which the contacts between East and West were almost nonexistent. Christian Europe held an embattled front against the Moslems in the Levant. But contact beyond, out into India, and on into China, was, during that period, virtually confined to the efforts of one or two Christian missionaries to reach the court of the Mongols. When Marco Polo, in the thirteenth century, gets a job as the secretary to the Mongol Great Khan, who at that time was also Emperor of China, and writes his reminiscences, he is obviously writing for a European audience whom he does not expect to believe most of what he is telling them. All echo of this remote kingdom of immense wealth and civilization has dropped from European consciousness. It is almost like tales of travelers from the moon and, when you read Marco Polo's text, you have the impression that he is forever adding a footnote, saying: I know you will not believe this, friends, but I assure you it is true. And, of course, Chinese society was perfectly fabulous to him and to his audience. At that time, the material civilization of China far outstripped anything that Europe could boast. So did that of many other Oriental countires. Their culture was at a higher level and their riches were much greater than those of Europe. They lavishly enjoyed the things which people of that time—or perhaps any time —valued most—gold and silver and precious stones, aromatic spices, wonderful damasks and brocades, scented woods, exotic flowers and fruits, carpets, jade, alabaster—all the attributes of wealthier, more developed and more civilized communities.

And yet, when Marco Polo made his journey, Europe was on the threshold of a decisive change which has differentiated the West from any other part of the world and which ensured that when contact between East and West was re-established in the sixteenth century, it would be of an explosive and revolutionary kind.

There has been a tendency in modern historical thought to look for the explanation of events in predetermined physical conditions—in resources, geography, class structure—and to plot on this basis a graph of human development which can be expressed in scientific terms and general propositions. One such example has been quoted. The Greeks, possessing too narrow a material base for agriculture, are forced to develop trade, and as traders evolve a middle class and democratic institutions.

But this method seems to leave out the other characteristic of history—either of peoples or of men—the characteristic of being uniquely and irreducibly themselves and, as it were, wearing their general laws and scientific categories "with a difference." It is no doubt an important fact about Shakespeare that he was a bourgeois poet of a late Renaissance period. But it is quite as important that he was Shakespeare.

The more one looks at the historical record, the more it seems that some events are irreducible, and that some nations simply do not display behavior which can be wholly analyzed in predetermined and explicable terms. They play their part more in the spirit of the genius or the poet. They are uncomfortable subjects for the systematizer or the proponent of general law.

So it is with the explosion of Europe in the sixteenth century. Up to that time, the tempo of history had tended to follow a steady rhythm. The rise and fall of civilizations—"vaster than empires and more slow" —had brought catastrophes and cataclysms but society was rarely changed in depth. The alternations of stars and seasons governed men's lives. A quiet recurrent cycle prevailed once the fevers of court and camp were left behind. But since the sixteenth century, the speed of human change has been revolutionized. A dynamism unknown before in human history enters the world as the first Portuguese boats nose their way round the African cape. The old rhythms of mankind give way to a rising tempo and a feverish activity. Not only dynasties change and fall. The foundations of existence are recast.

The agent of these changes—Renaissance Europe— emerged from its isolation from the East in a state of violent flux. In Asia, the old order was virtually unaltered. The new meeting—unlike the old—was not of like with like. Asia was confronted with something completely alien, completely unexpected, completely inexplicable, and from their point of view, quite extraordinarily destructive.

During the five or six hundred years when contact ceased there had, of course, been great changes in the East. Two or three empires had risen and fallen in the north of India and by the fifteenth century Moslem invasions from the North had established a Moslem overlordship over most of the land. In China the Sui and Tang dynasty ended one period of partition in the empire, another dynasty, the Sung, restored unity after the fall of the Tang. The Sung fell in turn and after a further period of partition, the Ming expelled the Mongol over-lords. But underneath these changes of dynasty or im-perium the major institutions remained intact and there was little modification of the basic way of life of Oriental people. For example, Buddhism, a religion of great pu-rity and of great missionary activity, arose in India, and spread to China. Nevertheless, by the fifteenth century, Buddhism had been practically wiped out in India, and had been confined in China to the remote regions, and was strong only in Ceylon and the fringe of southeast Asia. What had happened in both India and in China had been the restoration of the original, indigenous re-ligious systems. Confucian philosophy in China and Hindu thought in India reasserted their official pre-dominance.

Even where, as with the Moslem invasion of India, a new pattern of religion had been imposed, it left many of the basic religious attitudes unchanged. It did not touch the whole concept of the theocratic state. All men's activities, however practically secular, were the-oretically of a religious character and the purpose of human life was to conform to the great religious cycle of which night and day, the seasons, agriculture, birth and death were all manifestations. At the level of govern-ment, this attitude to existence was naturally expressed in the religious or semireligious character of the Emperor who ruled autocratically as regent of God.

Even if the content of dogma changed, the structure of administration did not. Akbar, Mogul of India, experimenting in universal religion or Aurungzeb, his fanatical Moslem grandson, relied on the same system of viceroys and tax-collectors as a great Buddhist predecessor, Asoka, had done. In China, dynasties received the "Mandate of Heaven" and lost it again but the change of ruling family left the governmental forms untouched. The Emperor, with his religious attributes and functions, ran a very large empire by means of a large bureaucracy, good communications and a delegation of powers to provincial viceroys. Corruption and invasion weakened the system. Victory and good government restored it. But its forms were unchanged.

Least of all had there been any change in the basic economic structure of the country. Both India and China were vast self-supporting communities, in which agriculture was the basic wealth, the land tax the basic form of revenue, and in which trade was confined to the luxuries and the unessential elements of life.

Thus, although there had been changes in dynasty, and catastrophes of war and invasion, droughts and famines, and religious movements of both a missionary and a militant kind, the basic structure of the Orient was not much changed between the time of the old contacts with Rome and Byzantium and the new incursion of the West.

If we compare this unchanged rhythm of Oriental life

with what had been happening in Europe meanwhile, we can measure the extraordinary explosiveness of the West's impact upon the East, when, after the sixteenth century, Western peoples reappeared, and reappeared in strength.

Taking the three spheres of life—philosophy, government, the economy—let us now see what had been happening in Europe. In the first place, the development of Christianity led Europe away from one of the abiding elements in Oriental religion—the quality of otherworldliness. Once the various gnostic heresies had been overcome, the trend of Christian thought was away from the belief that this world is unimportant, or an illusion, or bound by any absolute fatality to an unbreakable wheel of destiny. On the contrary, Christians tended to see the world as a testing ground, a creative area in which men could prove themselves and try to find out the dynamic purposes of God.

From their Jewish heritage, Christians had received the idea of God's purpose in the world being made known progressively in history. Man's record, therefore, was not simply a fatality or a succession of meaningless events. It was more like a drama, a drama in which a part was played out in time by both God and man. Time itself therefore became important. Time was something which you could not neglect. Time was not an illusion. Rather it was the theater, the stage, upon which the Divine purpose would be displayed. And to this religious inheritance we owe a basic concept of our modern world—one which, in spite of all our disillusions I do not think we are rid of, indeed, I hope we shall never be—and that is the idea of progress. Progress, which is a concept alien to Oriental civilization, came from the Jews, with their insistence upon the purposefulness of history, into the main stream of Christianity.

Another divergence from Asian thought came about in the Western approach to the individual human being. The Greek concept of a citizen with rights and the Jewish concept of the sinner with personal responsibility held in embryo the belief in personal individual freedom which appeared for the first time in history in the West. Again, in this notion of personal responsibility and of each soul being called to take its part in the Divine drama there is inherent some notion of equality. And this equality suddenly ceases to be an abstract idea and becomes potentially a flaming political issue when, for instance, in those pictures of the last judgment that you find in the parish churches of England, you see painted up on the wall a cardinal and a king in Hell, and a poor man going to Heaven. Here, fiercely dramatized, are the religious roots of the idea of equality, the basic metaphysical equality of all men before the throne of God—and, just in parenthesis I would add of all women too, because in the Western dispensation women are allowed souls as well, and that, I have always felt, is a remarkable step forward—but this is a digression.

Now, the notion of spiritual equality was bound to have a great effect upon politics, and it has been one of the underlying elements in the development of constitutional government. The idea of the government itself being under law, and the idea of all sections of the community enjoying freedom and responsibility to take part in government are the essence of our constitutionalism and much of it must be traced back to antecedent metaphysical ideas.

The economic transformation of Europe in the high Middle Ages—like the growing commercial activity of the Greek city states—played its part in developing the political consciousness of the merchant class. It was in the wealthy trading cities of Italy and the Low Countries that the first attempts at representative government were successful. But, as with the Greek merchants, the economic explanation must be balanced by the influence of dominant ideas. There seem to be three ways in which the distinctive cast of mind of European man influenced the transformation of society during the centuries of separation from Asia. In the first place, the underlying ideas—already noted—of personal responsibility and metaphysical equality gave the upthrusting groups of merchants and entrepreneurs some support in the general temper of society. They were not, as in a static and

(33)

completely closed hierarchic society, working against the grain of every preconceived idea among their fellow citizens.

In the second place, they were aided by the unique development, in Western Christianity, of separate religious and secular power. Other great civilizations have tended towards the coincidence of the two powers, but in Europe, where man had been bidden "to render to Caesar the things that are Caesar's, and to God the things that are God's," there was a large loophole for freedom and for differentiation in society, because power and authority were never concentrated at a single point.

In our day we have seen the appalling consequences produced by the concentration of power and we are not likely to underestimate the supreme significance of this division of power which was built into the foundations of Western society. In its most typical form in the Middle Ages, in the fight for supremacy between the Pope and the Emperor, it gave all manner of free cities and corporations and guilds the chance of playing the one authority off against the other, and of establishing their own independent jurisdiction; in this way Western society avoided the dominant political form of the Far East and India—the single theocratic order. On the contrary the political system was already loosened up as it were, the centers of power were already diversified. This decentralization enabled the concept of differing rights and of different types of authority to take root in men's minds. In other words, it enabled the pluralist society to develop. And, as one might expect, this society of a pluralist character, which did not fit into a single theocratic mold, proved to be of infinitely greater dynamism and growth than societies set firm in a single pattern.

Then there is a third sense in which the cast of Europe's mind caused a profoundly different development in West and East. At this point, our arbitrary divisions between philosophy, politics, and economics break down and Europe must be considered as a single dynamic process. As we have seen, the resources of Europe towards the end of the Middle Ages were, by comparison with Asia, poor. They covered a smaller geographical range. They included almost none of the most prized commodities of the day—gold and precious stones and so forth. (One can recall that Europe at that time was—like the Roman Empire—running a perpetual deficit with Asia in its balance of trade.) The merchants of the day were, therefore, in purely material terms at a disadvantage compared with their wealthy counterparts—Arabs, Indians, Chinese. Yet they became the founders of a new class and a new order—entrepreneurs, forgers of the industrial revolution.

It is true that the voyages of discovery of the fifteenth and sixteenth centuries provided an enormous material stimulus in the form of legendary bullion from South America. Yet this wealth was the ruin of Spain as well as the making of the Low Countries. We have therefore to look for more than purely material explanations.

It is at this point that what one could call in shorthand Europe's stamp of mind becomes relevant. Among all the variety of explanations for the immense head of physical and mental energy which was banking up behind the bursting-out of Europe all around the world in the sixteenth century, two should be singled out. The first was intellectual curiosity. However unworldly and ascetic were some aspects of the medieval church, the central teaching of Christianity had not deviated from its Jewish heritage. Time and the world were not illusions. They were the raw materials of man's struggle for perfection. What happened in time had significance and the material universe could show forth the glory and the will of God. The Renaissance restored the old Greek curiosity in material things as such and generated a passion for exact knowledge which was the forerunner—in such observers as Leonardo da Vinci—of the scientific revolution.

Yet earlier societies—the Greeks above all—had made considerable discoveries about the universe. But they had not used them to manipulate material things by applying science, through machines, to raw materials. Desire for wealth is not the whole reason for the industrial revolution. Oriental merchants and bureaucrats piled up huge fortunes but their capital went into jewels and concubines, not more factories and machines. One decisive reason for the rise of industrialism in the West was the Puritan tradition which combined the idea of religious vocation with hard work in workshop and countinghouse and allowed men to see virtue in accumulating vast fortunes and then in not spending them on worldly temptations. Capital ceased to be for enjoyment. It became the instrument of further work and the crucial capitalist cycle of saving and development was set in motion.

Thus in every field of human activity, the Europe which thrust itself out over the world after the sixteenth century was a new phenomenon among political organisms. Its religion was becoming this-worldly. Its trading governments were either in the first stages of limited democracy—as in Britain and Holland—or, as in the case of France, were mined with philosophical ideas preparing to blow despotic government to the skies. Any idea of a single theocratic civilization had vanished with the coming of the Reformation, leaving a group of strongly competing nation states. And the economies of the main trading communities—once Portugal and Spain were outstripped—were tending toward an entirely new type of organization—the industrial system. In the meeting of East and West, like no longer met like.

European society, in spite of its material inferiority, suddenly took on a power of growth and change and dynamism, for good and for evil, on whose wave we and the whole world with us are still rushing along.

Before we look at its impact on static Asia, it is important to remember that the dynamism and the growth and the immense activity of this society, had, like all human activities, its good and its bad sides. In other words, all this energy could be used on the one hand for great creativeness, and for the great growth, but on the other, for appalling destruction. The figure of Faust is, after all, one of the archetypes of this new phase in Western society, and, if you remember his career, it was one of great excitement, discovery, and momentum, but he very nearly lost his soul. The myth is typical of the kind of energy that was released in the West. On the one hand, it made for a human splendor, for growth, excitement, and capacity on a unique scale, but on the other hand, it contained within it forces of aggression and destruction, with which we are still living and of which we cannot by any means yet see the end.

On the side of creation and progress, the West gives us individual freedom and the concept of constitutional government. It has a living spirit of free inquiry, of scientific curiosity, and of humanist idealism. In the economic field it has given us the application of science to raw materials in industry, and through industry, at long last, mankind has seen the first possibility of moving the great mass of people on from the conditioned wheel of work and poverty. All these things have been accomplished, all these things stand to the credit of the immense outburst of creative energy in the Western world.

But for every high, creative, and promising achievement we have brought into the world, we have cast as dark a shadow. It is essential for us to realize this double-edgedness of our performance. We tend to think only of the good. We show insufferable complacency. We lecture Asian nations on their international behavior. We fall into attitudes based upon the most pretentious and unsubtle habit of dividing every issue into black and white and claiming the white for ourselves. All this is death to our relations with Asia, where we must show a decent humility and perspective or lose all influence and respect.

Now let us look at this sharply contrasted picture of light and shade. Against the political vision of free, constitutional government, we must set the excesses of nationalism. Nationalism is intimately connected with democracy. Nationalism in our modern sense was unknown in the East. All affairs of state and public policy were settled by the dynasty. The mass of people had no particular concern with either government or state affairs, even if in wars and invasions they often suffered the consequences. In such conditions, there are no motives for identifying yourself with the State in the same intimate way as you do, say, with family or clan or tribe. This dissociation can be illustrated, for example, from the wars of the ninth and tenth century in northern India; at that time, northern India was divided into a great many small states, under the Rajputs. But, owing to the caste system, none of the lower orders, the peasants or the artisans, had any part in government, or indeed, any direct part in the fighting either. The result was they were never personally concerned with the quarrels. Dynasties came, dynasties went, but the ordinary peasant and the ordinary townsman simply carried on his traditional life as best he could. Under such conditions, nationalism in the modern sense does not develop.

In the West, where the effort was made to associate more and more sections of the population with an active part in government and a responsible role in the community, the sense of belonging together within the state could develop. It could grow into creative patriotism. It could also become an aggressive and narrow nationalism. In the West, unhappily, the development of nationalism has run amuck to become the curse of the world. How else can one describe a force which has plunged the world in this generation into two worldwide and total conflicts, and which, in its course through Asia, has spread the spirit of collective aggression and reared up the nation state into the image of a Moloch swallowing up all its children's rights and interests?

Let us take another instance of the ambivalence of the Western achievement. Our spirit of scientific inquiry and our rationalism have not only cleansed large sectors of human endeavor from the paralyzing fears of fetish and superstition. They have done so without any necessary threat to a truly religious or spiritual concept of life. To believe that the whole of nature is orderly and gives expression to laws which may be uncovered by human reason—which is the underlying concept of science— is entirely compatible with the religious approach to life. But, in the Western world, so-called scientific thinking has often meant a complete wiping-out of the extra dimension of religious purpose and of religious faith in men's lives. It has left either an unthinking materialism or a vacuum of faith, which, more recently, has in some quarters, been invaded by an organized and philosophic materialism, in the shape of Communism, coming in to fill the void.

Again, our industrial system, which has gone so far and can go much further to meet the basic, grinding necessities of existence, was, nevertheless, in its early stages, pressed forward with a ruthlessness of exploitation which created its own reaction in Communism. In our own day it has, moreover, created problems of mass society and the mass organization of human beings, which seem, under any order of society, free or regimented, to threaten the opposite Western idea of the free individual and the creative citizen.

But perhaps the supreme ambivalence of our society lies in the fact that the Western world has produced, to some extent under the pressure of the same ideas and the same head of energy, two sharply opposed versions of modern industrial society. The sovereignty of the people—in the sense of responsible participation by citizens and government in their interests—is the aim of Western constitutional government. But sovereignty of the people has also been twisted by Marxism to be the divine right of the majority—who are workers and proletarians —to establish state dictatorship and give all power to the Party because in a mystical sense it *is* the will of the people. The forms of ancient despotism have been revived—the concentration of power, the imposition of a single philosophy of life, the subordination of the individual—and all this is done in the name of supposedly modern concepts and with the aid of undoubtedly modern scientific and industrial techniques.

Thus out of the West come two choices for Asia, two roads towards modernization, both propelled by the enormous energies of the last five hundred years.

Now let us look at the impact of these energies upon the Eastern scene. It very much resembles that of a highly destructive hurricane. If you take three great societies of the East—India, China, and Japan—and study the impact on them of the Western way of life, you will see the extent to which we have taken them, as it were, by the shoulders, and shaken them with such violence that little is left intact of their traditional structure. Now we stand at the end of the period during which their traditional ways have been so weakened that there is virtually no looking back towards the static, fixed, Oriental past and the only choice left open is under which form Asia will take the Western medicine of modernization and industrial growth. This choice will be the theme of the rest of this book, but, to round off the historical record, I would like to describe briefly the way in which our Western battering ram has attacked and shaken India, China, and Japan.

The fate of India under the impact of Western outward expansion was to come completely under the control of one Western power. They say that the British acquired their Commonwealth by absence of mind (and I sometimes think that they may be losing it the same way). Certainly as far as India is concerned, the process by which political control was transferred to the British was not part of a long-drawn-out and determined scheme of imperial conquest. One of the chief reasons why British control was established was the weakness of India itself. The structure of the Indian administration was beginning to totter after the fall of the Mogul Empire in the eighteenth century, and commercial rivalry between two colonial powers, Britain and France, led the British and the French to back rival kingdoms in India, in order to get trading concessions for themselves. Having begun to play dynastic politics, the British found that, in fact, they had to control all the kingdoms that had supported their rivals, and when they had thrown out the French, they found that large sections of India had almost by default come under their direct control. Some ambitious British viceroys there were who forcefully and purposefully extended British dominion, but the main transfer of power was to a great extent a by-product of trade. This fact, however, did not mitigate the effects of the process. By the mid-nineteenth century, the effective administrative control of India was in British hands.

British rule had in some ways a beneficial modernizing effect. It brought into an Asiatic country concepts of modern administration which, if a modern economy is to be built, are essential. At the same time, some of the bases for a modern economic system—communications, railways, irrigation—were laid and the beginning of industry was, if not encouraged, at least not actually stopped. So much for the gain. But at the same time, bringing India into contact with the highly developed industrial system of Britain did mean the collapse of its old economic structure. An earlier balance had existed

(44)

—admittedly at a very poverty-stricken level—between the peasant producing the basic means of the community and the artisans providing consumer goods from their own handicraft for small local markets. The coming of industrial goods from the workshops of Britain meant the destruction of the old handicraft structure in India.

And, in the ideological field, the British impact had a multiple effect. Western concepts streamed in, carried by administrators and missionaries—Christian values, humanistic ideals, rationalism. At the same time there was a growth of nationalism of the Western form. This movement was not only stimulated by the desire to get rid of the British. It also led tragically to a new vicious spirit of rivalry and intransigence between the Moslem and Hindu communities of India.

Last of all, contact with the West stimulated a reaction in the shape of a recovery and revival of Hindu thinking and of the old religious traditions of India. Gandhi, the apostle of Indian independence, was heir to this spirit. It is now alive in his successor, Vinobha Bhave, who is conducting the land reform movement —Bhudan.

To sum up, the British occupation caused in India a very complex series of ideological reactions. It led to the destruction of the old economic structure. It gave the first framework of a modern administration and the first taste of representative government. We have not seen the end of the upheavals the incursion caused. But one thing is certain—there can be no return to the old static theocratic society of traditional India.

Much the same process has been at work in China, although no European power directly took over the Chinese. For one reason, the Manchu Empire did not collapse in the nineteenth century, although it was undermined. For another, there were so many rival European powers in the field that no one of them was strong enough to take over from the other. And also, by this time, the Americans had entered the trading field, and would have nothing to do with the old exclusive patterns of colonial trade and conquest. They insisted on the establishment of the Open Door. The Open Door doctrine said, in effect, that every trader should be free to grab what he could, but that no one was to grab everything —even by arrangement with the Manchus—a fine doctrine for the traders, though not necessarily for the Chinese.

Yet, in spite of the fact that no Western power took over the government of China as such, nevertheless the effect of the Western impact was to undermine the whole basis of traditional Chinese society. Christian missionaries weakened the old Confucian concentration of authority in family and throne. Western political ideas— of republican government and active citizenship— surged in to discredit the dynasty and remove "the

Mandate of Heaven." The old agriculture and handicrafts of the villages were destroyed by the coming of Western goods, which broke up the local industry and established a new modernized economy in the coastal ports. It can in fact be argued that China's ordeal was worse than India's, for India gained a hundred years of orderly administration and inherited in 1947 a functioning state and civil service, whereas China was left to drift like a sailless junk, its old equipment destroyed by the West but with no new machinery installed. The drifting lasted from the Opium War of 1839 to the Communist victory in 1949.

Now we turn to Japan, whose reaction was totally different. First the Japanese excluded the West completely for two hundred years, and then, on the old principle, "if you can't beat 'em, join 'em," they contrived, in an incredibly short time, to transform their old static and despotic government into the semblance of a modern political democracy. By a tour de force, unequal probably in the history of economics, they built an entire modern economy on the basis of only one raw material, silk. Thus equipped, they embarked upon the chief game Europe seemed to have taught them—aggressive imperialist trade and war. Yet, in spite of this different reaction, the Western impact on Japan resembled that on India or China, for it swept away forever the old economic system and political structure.

So this enormous battering ram of the West, wherever

it hit, destroyed the old order. Whether it took over a country completely, as in India, whether it merely disintegrated the regime, as in China, or whether it stimulated the local people to put up a Western form of government—whatever it did, the old order passed almost without trace.

We are now living in the phase during which it will be decided—for we do not know how many hundreds of years—in which direction this disturbed and shattered Asia will move. We are living in a time of maximum ideological and revolutionary turmoil in the Far East. We are far, far removed from the distant period of contact between old and like civilizations. We have passed the period when a new incredibly creative and aggressive Western way of life came in to break up the old Eastern structure. We now face the question of what version of modern society, evolved in the West, the Asian peoples are going to adopt. Our own direct Western control is now all but removed, and, if one may make a digression, removed because, fundamentally, we cannot combine an imperial and a democratic system. When men talk about the disappearance of the Western colonial system, they sometimes forget how much of its disappearance has been due to the fact that basically Western people do not believe in it themselves. Before our own ideas of education had carried the ideal of national independence to the East, there were groups of dedicated people all through the West who were fundamentally opposed to the colonial system. In fact, in the United States, the West witnessed the emergence of a nation whose whole significance consisted in throwing off the colonial pattern and declaring the freedom of man.

In this period, then, when direct Western control has been removed, we must ask ourselves whether, having landed Asia in travail, we have nothing more to give, and nothing more to offer. Must we now say that this whole chapter of intense contact between East and West has come to an end? Or do we try to evolve positive policies of a political, economic, and indeed a moral and religious kind in order to bind our civilizations together?

Part of the answer lies in the fact that not having a policy will not spare us from interaction and contact. However much we in the West might wish to be isolated from the Asian crisis, however much we might wish to say that Asia was beyond our concern, modern science, technological change, and the whole shrinking of the world have made such an attitude impossible. To adopt it would simply substitute blind contact and hence collision for the possibility of a constructive approach.

Another reason for evolving a policy is surely a sense of moral responsibility for a situation which our intervention has so largely created. But there is a third reason for positive effort. If we have no constructive ideas, then, by default, the other version of the Western way of life, which is Communism, may become the decisive form of Asia's modernization. Such a development would be tragic for the West, and it would be an enormous tragedy for Asia as well. One of the most stimulating and hopeful aspects of the phase into which Asia is now entering is that, in spite of all the battering Asian societies have suffered at the hands of Western peoples, and in spite of their deep and justified resentment at the old colonial system, the fact remains that Western intervention has been an instrument whereby hopes of personal freedom have overtaken the old despotisms, and the prospect of economic advance has appeared in place of the old static devastating poverty of the masses. Although we of the West have much to be ashamed of, in the blindness and aggressiveness and pride of what we have done, it would be a great error if we now went to the opposite extreme and thought we had no contribution to make. There is nothing that the Asiatic peoples want more or fundamentally need more than the personal political freedom which their own civilizations, however stable and magnificent, have never known, and an economic advance which will give them elbow room in which to enjoy it. I think we can help them, and I hope we shall try.

PART

2

ALTHOUGH, certainly, man does not live by bread alone, a good part of the time he does live by bread—and here we must look at some of the economic problems created by the impact of our Western way of life upon Asia, above all, on the three great communities of Asia—Japan, India, and China. I should have liked to devote some attention to the fringe countries of southeast Asia, which lie between the giants. But if something has to be excluded, southeast Asia is a reasonable choice for omission not because these smaller countries are not of great interest in themselves but because their fate will be decided by the great decisions taken by their powerful neighbors. To a certain extent, this has always been true. Much of the cultural and political influence at work in southeast Asia has emanated either from India or from China, and the tendency holds good today: the great decisions will be taken in the big centers of power and population.

Now, from the economic point of view, the first and most interesting paradox is this: the intrusion of the Western world upon Asia has been entirely explosive and it has had a violent and destructive effect upon the local economies of Asia; yet, in spite of this, the Asian peoples are determined upon economic modernization. If you wish to discover one single overriding desire in all the countries of Asia today, it is to achieve a modern form of economy and to base it upon the economic techniques which have transformed Western life in the last hundred and fifty years.

The reasons for this are relatively simple. In the first place, it is a matter of power. This is perhaps the least attractive side of the past relationship between Asia and the West, but it is essential to understand it. The aspect of Western technology that impressed itself so strongly upon the consciousness of the Asian peoples was the overwhelming *force* of the new system breaking in from the West and carried by such tiny countries—for, after all, in relation to India and China with their millions upon millions, the small trading peoples such as the Dutch, the Portuguese, and later the French and the British, were not very numerous and, at first, not overly powerful. But, as the eighteenth century advanced, and with it, the West began to reorganize its system of power, with modern armaments and the backing of these armaments by strong industrial systems, Asia found itself outmaneuvered, outmanned, and outpowered by the West. The most convulsive reaction of Westernization in Asia occurred in Japan, and it is significant that its cause was Japan's determination to be equal to the West in military power. This was probably the decisive force behind the Meiji revolution of 1868.

Even the Indians, with their much more pacific philosophy, have felt, with the other states of Asia, that unless they industrialize, unless they pull level economically, then it is impossible to resist the strength and the outgoing violence of Western imperialism. We would say that that feeling is now out-of-date, but, as we well know from our own lives, ideas and, above all, fears, have a habit of lasting long beyond the point at which they have ceased to be rational. And, in Asia today, the fear of the outward drive of Western imperialism is a factor we have to bear in mind the entire time. One of the reasons why, for instance, a controversy has arisen about the form in which the Atoms for Peace proposals shall be implemented and atomic energy shared among the nations is the fear, in Asia, lest the present holders and wielders of atomic power in the West may in some way establish a monopoly and not permit Eastern nations to pull level.

The second reason for the Asian drive for modernization is the fact that for the first time in the history of mankind, communities have come into existence in the West which have virtually conquered poverty. I say "virtually" because even in communities as wealthy as the United States or Canada, obviously pockets of poverty still remain. But, broadly speaking, it is true to say that some of the modern Western communities around the Atlantic have achieved a standard of living which adds an entirely new dimension to human life. It means the certainty of food and health and shelter for all; it means a physical basis of life which is tolerable not just for the few but for the great mass of the population. The feeling, then, that poverty can be conquered is one of the great driving emotions in Asia today. Mr. Adlai Stevenson has called it the "revolution of expectation," and I think this is an excellent definition. All over Asia, in the past, the basic philosophy has been one of resignation. Men and women accepted the evils of famine, shortage, disease, drought—all the chances of nature—as facts that were fixed and unchangeable. Today, instead, as a result of incoming Western influence, the belief has arisen that something can be done about these evils, that the appalling fatalities, the grinding unbelievable poverty of the Asian world can be countered, that countries can expand and their economies grow. It is the change from fatalism to hope, from resignation to expectation, and this is perhaps the biggest revolution that a country can make.

These desires—to emulate Western power and eliminate Eastern poverty—are positive conscious motives for Asian modernization. But there is another, possibly even stronger reason, and that is that there is really no choice. Modernization must be achieved because Western influence has wiped out the old economic system and has vastly increased the birth rate. The choice now is: modernize or perish. Western intervention brought with it the destruction of the old balance in Asian economies. True, peasant standards all through Asia always lay very near the margin. It only needed a bad monsoon to produce drought and famine. In fact, in over four hundred years there was never one single year in which there was not a famine at some point in China, and about every fifty years came general famine.

In spite of this very low level of security, the life of the village community and the village economy was, nevertheless, maintained a little above the subsistence level by handicrafts, by the exchange of handmade goods in the local market. Now, it was this superstructure of the Asian village economy which was destroyed by the coming of the machine and by the arrival from the West of cheap industrial goods, particularly of textiles. Once well-made, tough, and extremely cheap cloth came flooding in from Lancashire, the hand-loom industries of China and India were hopelessly disintegrated and village life lost its old economic balance. The nineteenth century was therefore a period of considerable economic disintegration. For instance, in spite of all that was done in India to counter famine, in spite of the great extension in irrigation and the growth of means of transport which meant that, in a famine period, grain could be taken from surplus to deficit provinces, many economists argue that there was a distinct deterioration throughout the peasant economy of India simply because local markets and handicraft industries were so widely dislocated by the coming of Western goods.

To this must be added the impact of Western standards of sanitation and public health, which began steadily to reduce the death rate and to check infant mortality. An extraordinary spurt of population began in the nineteenth century in Asia and still continues. In India, the population is going up by four and a half million a year, in Japan by about a million. The most formidable increase of all may be occurring in China, where the total claimed is already six hundred million, and may be increasing, according to Chinese statements, by as much as two percent a year.

This enormous increase in the Asian birth rate means that no static economy could sustain the steady rise in the volume of people. It is only if the economies of Asia become as dynamic as their birth rate that there is any hope of avoiding catastrophic famines of the old type. Thus there is really no choice in this whole drive to modernize the economies of Asia; they must modernize or fail.

The only way we know in this world of making an economy dynamic is by moving on into the Industrial Revolution; this is the transformation Asia is determined to accomplish and this is what in fact it is setting out to do. But, as was suggested above, there are two methods by which this Westernization, or rather, modernization of the economy can be achieved—though, of course, this division is very oversimplified. We can make a completely stylized contrast and say that Asia can modernize either by way of free enterprise or by the way of totalitarian planning. But this is, to a great extent, an unreal antithesis. We can define the Communist system as one in which an omnicompetent state gathers into its hands all the means of production and all the levers of control in the economy and practices total planning. But when we examine the laissez-faire side of the antithesis, it is clear that there is no single type of free-enterprise economy.

In the Western world, no system is completely run by

private enterprise; and there is no economy, even though it calls itself Socialist, completely run by the state. The Western world has in fact experimented so far and so fast with various ways of mixing our mixed economies that it would now be very hard to define one single type of Western system. It is rather that we have a kind of spectrum moving from a relative degree of free enterprise combined with some government planning over to a high degree of government planning combined with considerable private enterprise. And the crucial difference between the totalitarian economy and the various forms of mixed economy may not lie in economics at all but in the political fact that totally planned economies have not so far been combined with political freedom whereas in the whole wide range of Western economies, political freedom is, with few exceptions, maintained.

Now, I am not what is sometimes called "a Chamber of Commerce Marxist." In other words, I do not believe that the free-enterprise system is the cause of liberty. I think rather that liberty is the cause of the free-enterprise system. Political decentralization, the plural society, and the rights of groups and individuals preceded the Industrial Revolution. To hold the opposite is in fact to subscribe to a form of strict economic determinism. Yet there is this link between political freedom and the mixed economy. Freedom is obviously endangered if all power is concentrated in the hands of the state. If political power is doubled by complete economic power, the result, to put it mildly, is placing temptation in the hands of commissars which they would be better without. There is, thus, a point in the spectrum at which excessive state planning and control run the risk of jeopardizing a healthy division of power and hence freedom itself. This is the relevant choice for Asia—not crudely between Capitalism and Communism but between a mixed economy compatible with political freedom and the total state.

If this is the choice, what are the factors that are likely to be dominant in the mind of Asia? The first thing one has to remember is that there is a deep-rooted and natural prejudice in the minds of many of the leaders of Asia when they consider what they call the Western type of economy—which, as a kind of shorthand, we will call capitalist. In most of Asia, if you say "capitalist," you also seem to say "imperialist," simply because, on the experience of the last four hundred years, such an association of ideas arises spontaneously. This prejudice has been created by real and inescapable historical facts. For instance, it is perfectly true, as pointed out before, that the impact of Western industrialism on the economies of Asia was in the first place destructive because it tore up the local structure of small-scale handicraft industry and with it that substratum of artisan skill upon which in Europe the Industrial Revolution was built.

Then again it is true to say that, owing to the free-trade theories prevailing at the time of Britain's imperial expansion into the East, the colonial areas, above all India, were not allowed, in the name of economic freedom, to establish the kind of tariffs behind which infant industries might have grown as they were growing at the same period in the no longer colonial United States; it was not, in fact, until about 1920 that the Indians secured a tariff sizable enough to protect the expansion of a really large textile industry in India. And, certainly, from the 1880's onwards, when Indian entrepreneurs, particularly the Parsees, began to attempt the creation of large-scale industry in India, they did so in the teeth of opposition from Lancashire; naturally, they acquired in the process a picture of die-hard Western opposition to the industrialization of their own country. Another instance may be quoted from the experience of the Tata family. These great Indian entrepreneurs pointed out that in the Bihar-Bengal area there was a concentration of both coal and iron ore entirely suitable for an iron and steel industry. But the family were compelled to launch the venture as a gesture of faith, with Indian capital. They received no support from London and no backing from the British government, whose officials did not consider that it was part of the role of a colonial regime to encourage local industrial development.

In China, in the nineteenth century, the determination of Western traders to open up the Chinese market to Western manufactures virtually removed the management of the Chinese economy from Chinese hands. The old system of trade controlled by the Emperor through Canton was abolished by the British by force of arms—after the Opium War of 1839–1842—and the concessions and special privileges then secured for Western commerce were wholly devised for the advantage of the foreign traders. A narrow Chinese class—the "compradores" or middlemen—made their fortunes as a result, but the benefits were not spread by any transformation of China's internal economy. On the contrary, as we have noted, the old village manufacturing system was destroyed with very little indigenous modern development to take its place.

Another disadvantage of colonial rule which still rankles in many countries—in Burma and Malaya, for instance—lay in the fact that foreign entrepreneurs under colonial occupation invested a great deal of capital in developing local resources, such as rubber, tin, or the Burmese rice crop, but the local population, while supplying the labor, received almost no benefit from the development because the sales and the profits and most of the coincidental managerial incomes were in fact absorbed by citizens of the colonial power. They felt, as a result, that their country was simply an area for foreign exploitation and that the economic activity going on around them was of no benefit to themselves.

Now this grievance was not altogether justified. Many Asian countries obviously gained very much from the phase of colonial exploitation. To quote a striking example, India's transport system was revolutionized during the British period of control. Irrigation work, too, was on such a scale that when India became independent, it had more irrigated land than any other ten countries of the world put together and all developed under the British raj. Moreover, the British contributed another factor of incalculable importance by introducing into India, with British education and later with British managerial methods, a trained Indian administrative and managerial class. Shortage of trained manpower is, indeed, the great gap in all underdeveloped parts of the world. We take it for granted, with our long tradition of education, that the supply of brain power will always be adequate to the tasks allotted it. But in underdeveloped economies it is probably the bottleneck of all bottlenecks in achieving rapid economic and social development.

The expansion of Indian education in the nineteenth century and the admission to the Indian Civil Service of Indian cadets on a footing of equality after 1920 helped to give the Indian community a group of superbly trained men capable of carrying the administrative burden of a federation bordering on three hundred and eighty million people—which is no small task. Admittedly, the advantages derived from colonial rule were greater in India, where the West provided a total framework of government. They were much less clear in China, where Western influence carried no direct responsibility and pulled down the old order without substituting anything new. Yet in China, too, the groundwork for modern skills was laid by Western educational influence. In fact, by an odd irony, many Communist administrators learnt their first lessons in modern methods at the feet of a missionary, often an American missionary at that.

But these incidental advantages are not today what Asia remembers of the colonial period. The picture that remains is one of disruption and exploitation. We may not like the fact. We may not think it wholly fair, but it is one of the given facts with which we have to deal. Therefore, when we try to test the Asian reaction to what we may call the free Western type of economy, we have to remember that, as far as Asians are concerned, the free economy came to them like the Greeks, bearing dubious gifts; and for some time to come the dubious gifts are likely to be remembered rather than the incidental advantages. Moreover, we have to remember that the prejudice has been enormously reinforced by Asia's experience at the hands of the first Asian nation to adopt a Western capitalist economy.

Japan contrived after 1868 to carry through a tour de force of modernization. A closed feudal regime was transformed into a modern, relatively highly industrialized economy in about three decades. And this was done on the foundation of a very inadequate supply of raw materials. In a comparatively short time, the old feudal classes were trained to become bureaucrats, technicians, managers; feudal families, such as the Mitsuis and Mitsubishis, used the old concepts of fief and clan as units for building giant industrial enterprises in the economy. Seen from an economic point of view, it far excels in brilliance of improvisation in the face of fearsome obstacles any other comparable industrial revolution. But, unfortunately, from the point of view of the rest of Asia and, indeed, of the West as well, the Japanese copied not only Western industrialization but also what they took to be the Western pattern of power and aggression. The first fruits of their modernization—which was achieved while the Western powers were scrambling very vigorously for control over the trade of China— was the decision to join in the imperialist game. Being very much nearer the spot, they could play with greater skill and, beginning with Formosa in 1895, they set to lopping off from China all territories that seemed detachable. Then after 1937, they moved in to impose imperial control over the whole of China.

Now all this was done in the name of modern capitalism and it enormously reinforced the rest of Asia in the feeling that there is some inherent link between an aggressive, imperialist policy with regard to colonial areas, and the existence of a capitalist system at home; thus Japan's sudden explosion into full-blown imperialism in a very short space of time confirmed all the earlier prejudices which had been created by the incursion of the West into Asia.

Now let us turn to another difficulty which confronts Asia in making its choice between a mixed economy on Western lines or totalitarian planning. It is that, on the whole, Asia has not produced the kind of entrepreneur or managerial type who helped to create the industrial revolution in the West. There is no time to go fully into the reasons for this, although one factor was mentioned above. The Calvinist glorification of work and saving and wealth not as a means to luxury but as the basis of further industry was a strong psychological factor in creating in the West the middle-class entrepreneur who was ready to take the long risks of industrialism, and to work creatively in the building-up of enterprises which would demand not only risk today and risk tomorrow, but a lifetime of work and control and creation. Now this type of industrialist seems to have been the child of the Protestant Reformation in the Atlantic world, and appears only rarely in Asia. There, merchants were much more likely to be engaged in commodity trading, or, where they were linked with nascent industry, they tended—as indeed some of them still do—to treat their very enterprises as commodities to be bought and sold in the hope of quick profit and quick exploitation of the market. They tend not to demonstrate that long, rugged determination to build up a full-scale industrial structure.

Now, admittedly these psychological obstacles to the growth of an entrepreneur class, though of great interest, are hard to evaluate. The point to remember is that in large parts of Asia, the industrialist of whom we think as the typical business manager or entrepreneur in the Western sense, has barely existed in the past and, even now, he is still hard to find. There are exceptions. Japan was able, as it were, to create him new out of the old cloth of feudalism and to do so, in part, through the discipline and the loyalty of the old Shinto system, the feeling of feudal or clan loyalty which, transformed into a new loyalty to the big firm, created the element of seriousness and long-term purpose. In India, some families, particularly among the Parsees, again appear to have developed a sense of a long-term commitment to their managerial responsibility. Of this spirit the Tata family, over four or five generations, are a remarkable example.

But beside them there are other well-known names in Indian industrial history (some of whom are, incidentally, in jail) who represent that other type of entrepreneurship which consists of rigging the market, cornering supplies, buying cheap and selling dear—in fact, doing all those things which, from time immemorial, have, shall we say, hardly endeared the merchant to the rest of the population.

This difficulty does not mean that private enterprise cannot be developed creatively in Asia. The experience of Japan, India, and the Chinese Treaty Ports proves conclusively that the managerial outlook can develop. But it does mean that one of the great challenges of the next forty or fifty years, particularly for Western firms hoping to establish or extend their operations in the East, is to build up among the recruits they will have to make in Asia—for no foreign firm can hope to survive unless the higher direction is solidly Asian—that type of managerial responsibility which has been the psychological basis of free enterprise in the West. The system could not have evolved solely on the basis of the profit motive. It had to be combined with the desire for long-term construction and with a sense of creativeness in building up the enterprise or corporation. Without this spirit, there is little sense of corporate responsibility or of the enterprise as a center of loyalty—loyalty to the management, to the workers, to the quality of the product, and hence to the consuming public. In other words, the profit motive alone is inadequate to produce what is now sometimes called "democratic capitalism."

But if Asia has lacked the tradition of the responsible entrepreneur, it has enjoyed another very ancient tradition—that of the loyal and faithful servant of the state— civil servant, bureaucrat. The age-old type of economy in Asia was the agricultural system based upon the self-contained village. But above the level of the village was a state system based upon an empire-wide civil service. The main task of the bureaucrats was to collect the land tax and to use this revenue for the state's irreducible purposes—mainly defense and some public works, the maintenance of roads, famine relief, and, in China, irrigation. Periods of greatness in the vast empires of India or China tended to coincide with periods enjoying an incorruptible and effective civil service. Whether it is King Asoka of the Mauryans, whether it is the Gupta Emperors or the Kushan Empire, or, later, the great Mogul Empire of Akbar, it is always true that their moments of glory coincide with a period of efficient, honest and incorrupt civil service.

The same phenomenon can be seen in China. The history of China is, broadly speaking, one of the waxing and waning of the great dynasties. The periods of high prosperity and achievement under the Tangs, the Sungs, the Mings and—the last of the dynasties—the Manchus, coincided with periods of good order, good heart, and incorruptible efficiency in the Mandarinate. Equally the times of disintegration were those in which eunuchs had taken over the palace and the Emperor's confidence and were using the administrative machine for extortion and corruption, thus offsetting and paralyzing the integrity and loyalty of the bureaucracy.

Thus while Asia lacks any strong tradition of the independent business manager and entrepreneur, it has enjoyed a long and in many ways great tradition of the loyal servant of the state. The great Asian countries have been at their strongest when their bureaucracies have been efficient and loyal and incorrupt. So we may say that in Asia there is a certain bias towards the civil servant, not of an ideological kind, but one springing from the long experience of its own history.

To this age-old bias must be added two events of recent history—the type of Western education received by many of Asia's leaders and the impact on Asia of the Soviet revolution. It sometimes seems as though most of the leaders in the new Asia—outside China—were educated at the London School of Economics. That is, of course, an exaggeration, but the fact remains that a great many of them spent the formative years of their education in Europe or the United States in the 1930's. No doubt many readers can cast their minds back to the 1930's and remember what they were thinking about the capitalist system in those days—particularly if they were young. The feeling was abroad that the system had to be radically changed, and the belief that a New Deal might be necessary or that the Labor Party might need to come to power was certainly not confined to those students that came to the West from Asia. (I remember sharing such feelings very strongly myself.) At that period, when so much of the crucial education of Asia's new leaders was under way, the feeling that socialism was a more just, a finer, a more admirable way of running an economy, was extremely strong, and it is not surprising that we find today, in India or Burma or Indonesia, men who are still socialists in that tradition of the 1930's and retain their conviction that "production for use, not profit" offers the best guide to economic policy.

Moreover, this bias is confirmed, in many Asian minds, by the deep religious and philosophical tradition of Eastern communities. Unlike the West, they have known no long period of separation of the spiritual and the material, of church and state, of the sacred and the profane. Their natural bent is to assume that all activities should conform to a moral or spiritual pattern. Socialism, seen as an idealized form of the industrial community, gains a natural acceptance in the Asian mind. Even where, as in the Gandhi tradition, industrialism is rejected as an evil, the idea that the economy should conform to religious inspiration seems to have more in common with socialism with its belief that the economy exists to serve the community, than with the mechanisms of capitalism —private profit and the motivation of material gain.

By a paradox, this antimaterialist outlook in Asia has been reinforced by the experience of an economy which in theory at least is entirely devoted to materialism. The Soviet experiment, projected and transmuted by Soviet propaganda, has greatly strengthened the notion that state control is the quick route to modernization. By suppressing the fact that there was any industry in Russia before 1914, and by denying that any Western assistance was forthcoming in the first Five Year Plan, the Communists have built up a picture of Russia's stupendous leap from primitiveness to the state of being one of the most powerful industrial nations in the world. The feeling that a nation can drag itself up by its own bootstraps, as the Russians have done, and the feeling that it can be done without any intervention or help from the West, have been powerful elements in Soviet propaganda in favor of Communism.

To sum up, Asian experience at the hands of Western traders and capitalists, Asia's own traditions of administration, its philosophical bias, and the impact on its thinking of Soviet expansion all tend to create barriers of mistrust towards Western free enterprise. If these were the whole story, we might expect Asia, inevitably and infallibly, to develop towards the totalitarian system. The drag in that direction is powerful indeed. But it is not the whole story. Nor is it a choice which the Western nations are powerless to influence. In this consists much of Asia's contemporary drama.

Now let us look at the strong pressures and currents flowing in the other direction. One of the strongest is the fact that the Russian experiment has now been in existence for nearly forty years. Moreover, a number of Asian observers have been to Russia and have seen and tasted life under a Communist dictatorship. There they have found that, far from representing the sense of brotherhood which underlies their idea of socialism, it denies and frustrates the creativeness and freedom of the individual citizen and smothers the aspiration of brotherhood under bureaucratic tyranny. Similarly, sympathy for the aims of the Communist revolution in China has not prevented visiting Indian delegations from criticizing the stifling lack of personal freedom which they have encountered in China.

Perhaps this is another way of saying that we should not underestimate for the peoples of Asia the attractiveness of personal freedom and the sense of living under the rule of law. If their old traditions are bureaucratic and dictatorial, much of their recent experience is not. Many of India's leaders were educated in England and there acquired, with the intensity of habit and self-evidence, the sense of what we know as freedom. A similar experience has come to many groups in Japan either by education or more recently by their life under American occupation. It is true that this direct experience is something of a wasting asset. The leaders thoroughly imbued with Western education and ideals are in their fifties and sixties. It is difficult to be sure what mentality will follow and it is in the next decade or so, while Western habits are still widespread, that the Western Powers need to formulate policies attractive to the new groups in Asia and establish new relationships adequate to the changed conditions of the world. But they should do so without discouragement, remembering that the ideal and practice of free government and the sense of living in a free society has proved formidably attractive to Asia, in spite of contrary traditions. We should be defeatists if we did not recognize and indeed cherish the power, as it were, of benign infection in Western freedom and the attractiveness of free society to people who genuinely come into contact with it. (I would add, in parenthesis, that this is the reason why in the last analysis the Russians have much more to fear from any raising of the Iron Curtain than we have, because, in spite of all the difficulties and frictions and uncertainties of our way of life, it is deeply attractive to those who can come and see citizens practicing personal self-determination at first hand.)

Similarly, a strong reason for the effectiveness of Communism in China is that China, unlike Japan and India, was never exposed so directly to the Western experience of freedom. During the late nineteenth and early twentieth century when India was developing with Western standards of education, law, and administration and Japan was being made over completely on a near-Western pattern, China underwent the interregnum of the collapse of the empire, followed by a period of warlordism which tore China to pieces until about 1925; then came the Nationalist dictatorship of General Chiang Kai-shek engaged in his struggle with Japan and his running, losing civil war with the Communists. In other words, China, unlike India and Japan, had far less opportunity of experiencing in any widespread or direct way what were the advantages and attractions of this untidy but creative personal freedom which we achieve in the West. It can be argued—and has been argued very persuasively by scholars such as C. P. Fitzgerald—that Communism, restoring state orthodoxy and bureaucratic control, and concentrating once more the aspirations and dependence of the people on the government, is in some way a direct and almost unbroken continuation of the old empire under the Confucian bureaucracy. What is certain is that there has not been in China anywhere near so complete a break with old tradition. As a result it is easier there than in India or Japan for the idea of total control to maintain its hold.

It is not only in politics that forty years of the Communist experiment have brought disillusion. Its economic performance, too, can now be questioned. There is no doubt about the achievement of Communism in building up with incredible speed the structure of heavy industry and accelerating, at whatever cost, the whole tempo of industrialization. But there is another total economic sphere in which Communism has, so far, achieved little striking success. This is the sphere of agriculture and of the reactions of the peasant. Russian agriculture has failed to expand in anything like the same measure as Russian industry. Every five or six years there is some kind of agricultural crisis which has to be met by concessions—later rescinded—on prices and private production. In certain sectors of the rural economy, for example, livestock conditions are still roughly those of 1928. In Eastern Europe, countries with agricultural surpluses, like Hungary and Rumania, have been driven under Communism to maintain food rationing. In short, it is easy to see that something has gone badly wrong in the handling of agricultural policy and in the government's treatment of the peasant.

Before trying to determine where the failure lies, I would like to point out that in the Soviet Union, although failure on the agricultural side is serious, it is not perhaps a complete and total disaster. There is virgin land to be ploughed up, there are unused resources, there is no great pressure of population. Russia, like the United States, is one of those areas in which resources are on the whole greater than the population pressing upon them. But if in Asia there is a failure with the peasants, if, in the two vast and comparable communities of Asia —China and India—the agricultural program falters, the result is not simply a setback. It is universal disaster, because it spells famine and death. There are no wide margins in either China or India, no virgin wastes waiting to be ploughed up. The agricultural problem, serious enough in Russia, is of desperate importance throughout Asia, where eighty percent of the people are still peasants and where the pressure of growing population on the land is irresistible.

Now let us go back to the question of why the Russians have failed in their agricultural policy. Although the origins of the creation of wealth are still very obscure to us, it does seem to be the case that the method by which an industrial revolution can be set in motion is by increasing agricultural productivity and then transferring the fruits of that productivity from agriculture to the development of industry. In other words, at some point the agricultural sector has to be squeezed in order to release the resources needed for capital expansion in industry. If a nation is fortunate—as we were, relatively speaking, in Britain—then innovators of genius like "Turnip" Townsend or Coke of Norfolk invent the rotation of crops and suddenly increase agricultural productivity to such a pitch that when the transfer of resources to industry begins, there is something left over for the farmers as well. The economy as a whole begins to rise. There is inducement to the farmer to increase his productivity because he does not feel that the entire increment that he is creating in more efficient agriculture is just being drained off to the factories and the cities.

But Britain is a remote example for Asia. There is one nearer home in Japan's highly efficient economic revolution after 1868. One of the bases of that revolution was a very drastic land reform. The old feudal landowners were expropriated, they received payment for their old holdings in bonds which were then invested in the beginnings of industry and they themselves were drawn into the new managerial positions. The peasant proprietors were helped by the State to introduce fertilizers and new agricultural methods, and it is estimated that something like a two-thirds rise in agricultural productivity occurred before 1900. Thus there was a margin of capital which could be taken from the land and put into industry, yet the farmer still felt he was better off. Moreover, the industrial revolution in Japan—as in Britain and in America—was to this extent a natural revolution in that the first industries to be developed were those responding to ordinary consumer wants—textiles and consumer goods of all kinds. The farmer could use his extra earnings to buy goods he needed and had an inducement to produce still more.

This is not to say that grave evils, injustices, and hardships were not imposed by the transfer of capital from agriculture to industry. But at least in the Western world and in the early days in Japan—before population outstripped resources again—there was a margin. But in Russia, industrialization has proved tougher and cruder. Owing to the theoretical formulations of the Communist program, it was decided that the State should develop heavy industry first; at the same time, the political decision was taken that since the peasant was politically a doubtful factor he must be kept under strict State control. He could not be encouraged to increase his own productivity on his own land. That might lead to independent thinking. He had to be collectivized and this policy, instead of raising agricultural productivity, lowered it. Then only by forced deliveries of grain from the peasant to the town could any surplus be transferred to industry and the use of force left the peasant even more un-co-operative.

In the meantime, the surplus that had been wrung from agriculture was turned into hydroelectric power schemes, into heavy steel mills and machine-tool plants —in fact, into producer goods so that, even if the Soviet farmer had had some surplus income to spend on manufactured goods, there was nothing he could buy. He might have bought a bicycle, he certainly was not going to buy a steel plant. He simply had no inducement to do better and has continued—hence the recurrent peasant crises—to do worse. This is an "inherent contradiction" in the Soviet system and one to which it has been brought basically by political decisions—by the desire to build up State power ahead of popular consumption and by distrust of an independent peasantry.

But in Asia where the industrial revolution lies ahead, and where the vast mass of people are peasants, an "inherent contradiction" in agricultural policy is not just a side issue. It can be decisive to the whole process of modernization and it now seems certain that in the next decade a most fateful duel will be fought out to determine what, in the conditions of Asia, is the best and speediest form of modernization. On the one hand, China will follow close on the Russian plan. On the other, India will attempt the way of freedom, peasant advance, and the mixed economy. Asia's future, perhaps the whole world's future, will be decided by the outcome of their competition.

One of the difficulties of interpreting the present Chinese scene is that reliable statistics are not available and such as there are are expressed in terms of proportions based on an unreliable base year. The United Nations Commission for Asia and the Far East, for instance, gives a series of the various kinds of statistical computations you can derive from published Chinese figures and shows how the result is different, depending upon which computation you make. This uncertainty must be kept in mind in discussing Chinese claims and plans. Now as far as we can make out from the Five Year Plan which was introduced in 1953 the emphasis is that of the earlier Soviet pattern. In other words, the peasant, being politically unreliable, is to be controlled. Having briefly enjoyed his land reform, he is now to lose the land again and lose it fast. For example, one forecast is that by 1957 virtually all Chinese farming households will be grouped in "producer co-operatives," which is just another word for a collective farm. Yet, all through this year (1955), the peasant has shown signs of protest at forced grain collections which leave him without enough margin to live on. There have been reports of peasant unrest in many parts of China, of protests at the tax collector who turns up in the name of the government, demanding grain for the city.*

At the same time, if one examines the Plan published in 1953, one finds that the major emphasis is placed upon heavy industry. The maximum expansion is in sectors such as steel-making, pig iron, electric power, machine tools. Top priority goes to the development of the An-

* An exceptionally good harvest in 1955 seems to have lessened the friction in 1956 and encouraged the Chinese government to press forward even more rapidly towards collectivization.

shan district into a new Pittsburgh. Some 85 percent of capital expenditure is for producer goods. In other words, the Plan gives first place to those elements which make up heavy industry (which incidentally help to maintain armies), and the consumer-goods industries must take their chance. The risk which the Communists in China face in following the Soviet pattern is that this method of squeezing the surplus out of the agricultural sector is not likely to increase agricultural productivity. The farmer is left with little inducement to produce more, for what he has is taken and in any case there are few consumer goods available. It follows that we may see in China—though, Heaven knows, prophecy would be out of place—a scale of peasant discontent and a degree of failure on the agricultural front comparable to the rural difficulties in Russia. And such difficulties in China could amount to a national disaster, for China, unlike the Soviet Union, suffers an unrelenting pressure of population upon the land and has little new land that can be brought under cultivation.

However, we have to remember that, one way or another, the nations of Asia are determined to achieve modernization and the Russian model at least shows how it can be done, at whatever cost. If there is no alternative, then Asia will no doubt follow the Communists and try to bludgeon its way through. The hope for more liberal methods lies therefore in the success of the

Indian attempt to transform their system by basically democratic means. In their first Five Year Plan the Indians put the major emphasis not upon industry but upon raising the level of agriculture. Something like 60 percent of all expenditures under the first Indian Plan were designed in one way or another to raise agricultural productivity and to increase the fertility and the enterprise of the countryside. What is more, the biggest emphasis in the social revolution in India has been put, not upon collectivizing the peasant, not upon forcing him into a pattern which permits the state to exploit him without redress. On the contrary, the Plan attempts, by means of widespread land reform and of village self-help, to raise the whole tempo of village life and to do it on a basis which has long been accepted in India—the basis of self-government and self-help at the village level.*

The Community Projects and the National Extension Service, which it is hoped by 1960 will spread right over India, aim at bringing together groups of villages—about two hundred villages make up each of the project areas—and then, by providing seed, fertilizers, tools, experimental demonstrations, under the supervision of trained village workers, hope to give the villagers themselves the incentive to bring their whole rural life into a state

* The Panchayat or village council is one of the oldest institutions in India.

of dynamism by their own action. The attempt is, in fact, the exact opposite of the pattern of collectivization. The state bureaucrat does not come and tell the village what to do. The villagers are encouraged and urged to decide themselves what should be done to raise their village and to give it an expanding productivity, without which any hope of saving India in the long run would be entirely vain. It is still too early to judge of success. Grain output has already reached in India—in 1955— the level planned for 1957. But two excellent monsoons helped in the process. Yet it is an interesting contrast that in 1955 all kinds of controls over the movement and selling of grain in India were removed, because the supply was so lavish, whereas, at the same time, rationing of grain had to be re-established in the cities of China. It may be that here was more than a freak of the weather and that what was demonstrated was the perennial failure of the Communists to conciliate the peasant and the possibility that, in India, much more imaginative and flexible means of agricultural revolution are going to have their effect.

Even so, we have to remember that the battle for capital accumulation—for that, basically, is what the industrial revolution is about—is far from settled in either country. The Communists may be risking success by their regimenting of the peasants. But the Indians run an equal though opposite risk. Both countries face a relentless rise in population, and there is a tendency that any increase in productivity may be largely consumed by the new mouths that come into the community. In a free society which, like India, is encouraging peasant self-help, one likely form of self-help is to help oneself to most of the extra fruits of new productivity, leaving little or no surplus for industrial development. Whatever the long-term political, social, and ethical consequences, a government aiming at rapid industrialization may have a decisive advantage, if it can use violent means to compel forced savings and to compel people to render up their surplus for central planning and central investment.

The Indians are committed to the belief that expansion can be achieved by democratic means and democratic persuasion, and by creating the dynamism of expansion from the bottom. The Chinese are equally committed to the idea that the process must be directed from the top, with total centralized control. So confident are they that they can squeeze out the surplus that they plan in the next decade to achieve a steel industry as large as Western Europe's. Indian planners are—and must be—much more cautious, and it may be that their slower rate of capital accumulation will give Asia's verdict to the Chinese method.

This is, then, the decisive duel in Asia. Although it is rooted in the fields and farms, it affects every other sector of the economy. If India can achieve the transfer of capital without coercion or any sharp extension of direct state control, then there is every chance that the present Indian intention to maintain a mixed and open economy will not be shaken. Private enterprise's function will be recognized and even though state enterprise will expand, it will do so by pioneering new fields rather than by taking over existing private ventures. Foreign capital will still be welcomed, and foreign participation in Indian enterprise. The general pattern may be "socialistic," as Mr. Nehru forecasts, but there will be margins and elbowroom and the political atmosphere will be free.

If, on the other hand, capital is not secured, if population outstrips resources and modernization is delayed, the Chinese pattern under total public ownership, public control and political tyranny will become Asia's norm. These are the stakes between India and China.

One may ask in parenthesis whether in this duel of the next decades, Japan will not play a decisive role. The first answer is that, given a resurgent China, Japan, whose civilization has always been in a measure derivative, will probably no longer exercise the influence it gained by being the first nation in Asia to modernize. The dominant Asian powers have long been India and China and this old pattern seems likely to be re-established now.

Yet Japan could clearly play a balancing role and if

its present economy were to collapse, another powerful blow would have been struck to drive Asia toward a totalitarian future. After the tour de force of the late nineteenth century and the imperialist adventures of recent decades, Japan, in spite of building a strong industrial structure and one of the greatest exporting systems in the world, still suffers from a fundamental unbalance of resources. Since 1945 the Japanese have lost forty percent of the territory they then controlled. The steady rise of population continues, yet millions more have been repatriated. The American occupation and the vast help of the American taxpayer have provided a temporary respite—and some lasting advantages, for instance, General MacArthur's land reform, which not only reduced tenancy to a tiny proportion of the Japanese people, but also increased the purchasing power of the farmers and added something like ten percent to the cultivable area of Japan—no small achievement in a country already so fully developed. Even so, the inexorable pressure continues and will become impossible unless Japan can find its place as a great trading nation and make up in foreign trade what it lacks at home.

It is estimated that, under the most favorable conditions, Japan will always have to import at least twenty percent of its foodstuffs and forty to fifty percent of the raw materials it needs for industry. Other nations are in something of the same plight—Britain, for instance, or

Western Germany—and with expanding world markets and a rapidly growing world economy, there is no reason for the exporting nations to find their plight intolerable. But, given any failure, any repetition, even mildly, of the world depression of the thirties, then the mixed economy of Japan would collapse and the attempt would certainly be made to try a Communist cutting of the Gordian knot.

The question we must now ask is whether we in the Western world, having given up colonial control, have any further interest in the Asian situation. Does it matter to us which method succeeds, does it matter to us if totalitarian methods are adopted? Or have we some stake in the possibility of developing Asia by techniques compatible with freedom and the mixed economy? It is my profound belief that we are concerned in the most vital way in the outcome of this great duel in Asia. In the first place, whether we like it or not, we are involved in the political challenge. India and Japan and the remaining Asian states are all, at the moment, opposed to Communism as an internal program. They make up the "uncommitted peoples" whose political weight in world affairs, particularly in such a forum as the United Nations, prevents the balance of power from falling decisively on the Communist side. Yet these nations know that if their present more liberal methods of modernization fail, Communism exists as an alternative—in fact, as the only alternative. Thus, if India and Japan fail in their attempts to preserve and expand the mixed economy, most of mankind will come to live under the totalitarian system and the pressure upon the West will become steadily more intolerable. Least of all can there be any surviving hope of creating a world community amenable to reason and the rule of law.

The West's economic interest is equally vital. Only if the world enjoys a growing and expanding market can countries such as Britain or Germany—quite apart from the question of Japan—hope to support rising living standards for themselves. In a static or shrinking world market, competition between exporters leads to impoverishment and dislocation. But the expansion of industry in such vast areas as India creates new demands and new outlets for manufacturers and traders everywhere. True, new opportunities would, no doubt, be created by Communist expansion but the Western powers have already experienced the uncertainties inherent in trade which is conducted as an arm of political activity. Trade dependence upon growing Communist markets could involve political dependence as well.

These motives of enlightened self-interest—political and economic—are so obvious that there is no need to expand them further. But there is one other motive which is perhaps not so self-evident.

The starting point is a moral principle—one of the most potent and significant principles of Western society. It is that, as members of a social community, we have responsibilities to our neighbor. The gifts with which the Lord has seen fit to endow us are not talents to be buried in a napkin. They are to be used for the benefit of those who are around us and for the community at large. We have expressed this principle in some institutions which may seem on the face of it remote from religious inspiration—for instance, progressive taxation—but nevertheless the fact remains that in the last hundred years it is the widening acceptance of social obligation—of rich for poor, of healthy for weak, of lucky for unfortunate—that has made our Western Community a tolerable and increasingly democratic society.

So far we have applied this principle of solidarity, broadly speaking, only within the framework of national frontiers. But now that we have invented the atomic bomb and the intercontinental missile, we have created a physical unity which goes far beyond frontiers. In the sense of physical nearness and neighborhood, all mankind is now a single community. The question is, therefore, whether the principle of solidarity which has saved our domestic community has any relevance to the new wide unity of mankind.

Before we answer this query, let us remember that the group of nations round the North Atlantic Ocean are the privileged aristocracy of world society. They live in areas which not only are the most pleasant to live in from the point of view of climate and temperature (consider that wonderful unearned increment of spring and autumn—try going somewhere where there is no such thing—see how you miss it)—but also possess the richest resources for industry and agriculture. Moreover, they feel little pressure of population upon these resources. All these are advantages to which, like the children of rich Victorian parents, we have been born. We are heirs to a range of resources and opportunities that today enables us, some sixteen percent of the world's population, to enjoy steadily about seventy percent of its annual income.

In short, we of the West, a group of nations including Western Europe, North America and the non-Asian British Commonwealth, are in fortune and resources the lords of the earth. We are as wealthy in relation to the rest of the world as was, say, Andrew Carnegie in relation to his steel workers. Thus in a world made physically one by our Western science we occupy the position occupied a hundred years ago by the privileged and the wealthy within domestic society. The problem is: do we complete the analogy? Do we recognize that we saved freedom in the West by sharing wealth and opportunity with the mass of people *within* the state and must now do the same with the masses across the frontiers whose poverty and hopes are, if anything, greater?

This ultimately is the ethical problem which our society has to solve. But our religious traditions do not leave us without guidance. We have, after all, given lip service for two thousand years—possibly with less than real commitment—to the idea that all men are brothers. Of course, if the Christian idea is wrong, if mankind is not a brotherhood, then all obligations may be held to stop at the national frontier. We can keep our seventy percent of the world's income until somebody else comes and takes it away from us. But if by any chance what we Christians have always been saying is true—that all men are brothers, and that the man who falls in the ditch can be of whatever color but we still have to behave like good Samaritans when we pass by—if that is the case, then we face a profound moral decision in our relations to Asia. For they are our brothers and, while we are the "haves," they, most decidedly, are the "have-nots." They are the men in the ditch.

/ Let us assume that the decision is made and that we recognize our moral responsibility to Asia. What follows? There can be no doubt about the availability of means to carry through our obligations. Estimates of Asia's needs vary but it is generally agreed that, at this stage, the countries could hardly absorb more than three billion dollars of new capital a year—the shortage of trained manpower is a severe limiting factor. But such a sum represents not even one percent of the United States' national income, let alone the incomes of its wealthy allies. Nor can we doubt that the inventive skill needed to organize such a program could be mustered by nations who have had to their credit the organizing of a great wartime coalition or such a peacetime adventure as the Marshall Plan. It is not means that are lacking. It is the political will to use them.

Yet if such a program were undertaken on a sustained basis, say, for the next four or five decades, during which the competition between Communist methods and those of the free mixed society will be most intense, there can be little doubt that India would receive the crucial reinforcement in capital and Japan the guarantee of expanding export markets which both need to get ahead of the pressure of population on their resources.

Nor would the victory be confined to the economic arena. The adoption of a long-term program for Asia would bring with it inestimable political advantages as well. The peoples of Asia still have a vision of the Western powers as imperialists and aggressors. The picture is no longer true, but you do not erase an age-old image simply by default. The speediest way to change it is to put another picture in its stead. If over the next fifty years—I suggest fifty years because, after all, our imperialism lasted four hundred years and this is the length of memory we have to counter—if, over the next fifty years, the Asian nations could come to depend upon Western help given generously, intelligently and cooperatively, to the tune of, say, one or two billion dollars a year, I think we should finally wipe out the picture of Western exploitation and imperialism, and, by doing so, we should have done more than by any other conceivable policy to preserve liberal and freedom-loving ideals in Asia.

Nor should we think of this achievement as being solely or mainly in Asia's interests—the majority of mankind live there and in this small world they will play a decisive part in determining the political coloring of the whole world. Therefore, I would say that underlying any policy of economic aid for Asia must lie the political aim of establishing with Asia the kind of world order without which life for all of us will be intolerable. Our stake is as great as theirs. It is the survival of freedom.

PART

3

WHEN we turn to con-
sider the political relations between East and West, we
have to admit that today, as indeed for the last hundred
years, they are dominated by the fact of nationalism.
Indeed, one could argue that the master institution produced in the political life of the West in the last six hundred years is the Nation State. It has drawn its strength
from many roots. First of all, it goes back to the tribe
itself and to the sense of protection which man, faced
with fear of an unknown and largely hostile universe, felt
from gathering together with his kin. In the protective,

co-operative group of clan or extended family he could defend himself against his neighbor, establish his control over hunting fields and fishing rights and generally carve out a small area of certainty and security.

Perhaps this tribal feeling is the deepest of all our aspirations. It is certainly one of the oldest. From the very beginning of organized political life among mankind the sense of belonging to one group and not belonging to another has been enormously strong. Then, as civilizations developed, the old feeling of the tribe or clan developed into the idea of loyalty to the clan chief and loyalty to the dynasty. History witnessed a whole series of dynastic states in which the sense of "belonging," in so far as it was felt at levels higher than the village community, was linked to the person of the king. But, admittedly, this positive loyalty of owing allegiance to one monarch was stimulated most fiercely in times of dynastic war. Patriotism was no doubt a high virtue but its strongest expression was often the readiness to maim and kill those who did not accept the same loyalties.

In our modern world these old, long-established, deep-rooted political institutions have taken a new and what I fear one can only call a more virulent form. The reason may partly be a matter of coincidence. Three states which, on a dynastic basis, were established most early in Western Europe also offered a unique coincidence of language and frontier. In Spain, in France, and in Britain, three of the first kingdoms to develop from medieval dynastic politics to what we would now call the modern Nation State, the linguistic and geographical frontiers overlapped to a degree which is far from usual in the world at large. A more usual pattern in human history has seen many different language groups ruled together by a single dynasty. This pattern was broken in Western Europe. The idea therefore grew up that a man who spoke the same language was a brother and fellow citizen and anyone who did not was an alien.

This extreme concept of solidarity by tongue has lain at the root of a great many troubles in Europe ever since the first crystallization of modern nationhood in Britain, France, and Spain. It has not only added a lethal edge to war. It is totally inappropriate to areas of mixed language such as the old Austro-Hungarian Empire, for example, where there was no possibility of making frontiers and languages coincide.

Nationalism has been further enhanced by the growth of democracy. If everyone has a right to participate in the political control of the State, then everyone tends to feel that there is far more at stake in the State than the fortunes of this or that dynasty. A citizen's own private and personal fortunes are involved in what happens to the community. His sense of oneness with his own society is inevitably reinforced, and democracy and nationalism grow together.

Last of all—and this is perhaps the most serious of all developments—modern industry has grown up and drawn the whole community into a web of production, trade, and commerce. Local differences in the economy vanish. A man's whole livelihood no longer depends entirely on the village or the valley, or a local type of agriculture. It is bound up with the fortunes of the national market. Each citizen shares in the economic interests of the state and the state becomes the representative of the total economic life and interests of the people. Trade is no longer a fringe activity conducted by a few merchants; trade is the life-blood of the nation and if the country cannot trade or prosper, the life of every citizen is exposed. Thus, as Professor Toynbee has pointed out with extraordinary vividness, into the old institution of the dynastic state, with its limited political loyalty, we have poured two enormously powerful molten-lava streams of political energy. One is the identification of the citizen with his stake in democracy. The other is the total identification of his interests with the industrial and economic life of the country.

The new wine in the old bottles has proved an intoxicating brew. The modern Nation State virtually admits no rule beyond its own, no interest beyond its frontiers, and no check, even theoretical, upon its sovereignty. And this, first produced in the Western world, was the instrument through which Western life has, in the last four hundred years, been carried out into Asia, and, as pointed out above, it came in a highly aggressive form. The spirit of nationalist aggression first came to the notice of men in the East in the shape of bitter national struggles between different trading groups, between Portuguese and Dutch, between French and British. Serious Eastern observers, accustomed to the "live and let live" policies usually pursued by earlier traders, particularly the Arab traders, were amazed and indeed disgusted to see that there was virtually nothing that a merchant of one European nation would not do to a merchant of another nation provided he could get rid of his competition. At the next stage of Western encroachment, the nations of Europe had developed their industrial strength, and national rivalry was now used as part of a pattern establishing colonial and imperial control over Asian lands. Indeed, one of the reasons why the Japanese excluded all foreigners for over two hundred years was because they had come to the conclusion that the merchants from Europe were always the entering point, the wedge, for the coming of political control exercised by a European nation. At the same time, although the impact of Western economic policies on Asia was in many ways progressive and dynamic, it also involved a large element of exploitation and the sacrificing of the interests of the local people to that of distant Western European nations; capitalism and exploitation, capitalism and imperialism, became synonymous in the minds of Eastern peoples.

Today, we have entered a new phase. Nationalism in the exclusive arrogant Western sense has become the guiding star of Asia. The habit of intense nationalism has been caught from us because Asians came to believe that this was the only way in which they could ever meet us on our own terms. For the last fifty years and more, Asia has been undergoing the type of national revolution which occurred a century or so earlier in Europe. The concept of the dynastic state has largely disappeared. In its place Asian peoples are enshrining the Nation State. The Japanese, for all their theoretical devotion to the Emperor, led the way. In India, the spirit of exclusive nationalism led to the tragic split between Hindu and Muslim in which religion served as the new determinant of nationalism and divided the subcontinent into two States. In areas like Kashmir, nationalism determines a government to impose its will upon a local people even if the local people are not particularly anxious to receive that form of political control. In Indonesia, Javanese nationalism suppressed a federal form of structure and imposed a unitary state.

But perhaps the most remarkable illustration of the

strength of this new nationalism that has swept Asia lies in the fact that it is proving in many ways stronger than Communism itself. I do not mean to suggest that nationalism, as such, is sufficient to counter Communism. We have seen in China how the nationalistic dictatorship of General Chiang Kai-shek was in fact defeated by the Communists. But the Communism of Mao Tsetung is a thoroughly *national* Communism. A first step after victory in 1949 was to send Chinese troops into areas such as Tibet, once loosely under Chinese national control. Another instance is the attempt to mobilize the overseas Chinese in southeast Asia in the interests of Communism. In short, China is following the example of the Soviet Union where Communism began as an international movement but has tended more and more to become subordinate to the interests of Great Russian policy. We can surely say that any force that is strong enough to master the great supernational ideology of the twentieth century must be a very formidable force indeed.

This development may mean that Communism has the best chance of exploiting nationalism to the full. But it also means that once we are confronted with a Communist revolution, we should not think for one moment that we are rid of nationalism. One need only cite the example of Tito in Yugoslavia and his long feud with his large Communist neighbor. Communism can exploit nationalism but nationalism can also penetrate and completely permeate Communism. One consequence, incidentally, of this development is to refute the Communist claim that Communism alone provides a basis for world order. When it comes to the crucial point, Communism becomes one more instrument in the hands of aggressive nationalism.

This frantic development of nationalism may have been set on its way quite inadvertently by us (the number of things that the West has inadvertently started is really startling), but it has now reached its climax with the attempt of virtually all states in the world to organize themselves on the basis of the Nation State. And, by history's greatest and potentially most tragic ironies, this worldwide opting for total, unfettered national sovereignty has come at a time when science and technology are making complete nonsense of any nation's claim, even the largest, to be totally sovereign and self-contained. Think of changes that have occurred in communications, in travel, in the whole organization of economic life in the last hundred years. They point in one direction only, towards a world so small and so integrated that it must find some form of social and political order which transcends all these supposedly sovereign units. We have reached the quintessence of nationalism just when, from the point of view of industrial, economic, and social organization, exclusive nationalism has become completely impracticable.

This is the profound political dilemma with which we are living and it is a dilemma not only of the West. It is a dilemma of East and West together and at this point there is not much difference between the problems that lie ahead for either sector. We can say perhaps that we in the West who have lived with nationalism rather longer are possibly less excited by it than those new nations in Asia or those emergent nations in Africa for whom nationalism is a new strong drink only tasted in this century. But from the point of view of any kind of sane world order, it is nonsense in West or East to suppose that all these various competing and anarchical sovereignties can prosper without any form of organization which transcends them, or any form of order which co-ordinates their activities and helps them to avoid the gravest forms of clash. The fact that the notion is nonsense does not, of course, mean that mankind is not going to attempt to perpetrate it. But nonsense it remains and potentially violent, dark, destructive nonsense at that.

However, the scale of the folly may now help to induce new ideas. Our grandchildren may look back upon this age and be grateful to the atomic bomb and the hydrogen bomb because they realize that in no other way could it be demonstrated to a blinded humanity just what folly its arrogant parochialism had become. If weapons can now blow up a whole continent, if even a quite limited use of modern weapons can extinguish the human species, then, clearly, men have some overriding interest in common, however unwilling mankind as a whole may be to admit this fact. Perhaps we need something as horrifying as the hydrogen bomb to startle our imaginations into realizing that in a world as close, integrated, and tiny as our world today, the uncontrolled competition of anarchic national sovereignty is a condition which, literally, we must overcome or perish.

So often before, we have said that we must overcome national rivalries or be destroyed. But, this time, there is a literal sense to the words. It is highly doubtful whether our planet could stand more than a certain amount of hydrogen warfare; this generation certainly could not, and it is even doubtful whether the human species as such could either. So we face, at the moment of our extremest nationalism, the fact that it is the highroad not simply to disaster but probably to extinction. We may hope that this fact will dawn upon more and more of us (although, I am afraid, at present it seems to dawn every time there is an atomic test and "undawn" the moment the test is over). However, let us suppose, as a supreme act of faith, that the dawn stays and develops into a broad day of intelligence. Then I do not think there will be much doubt about the task that lies equally before both East and West. It is to devise those institutions—they can be minimum institutions—which transcend national sovereignty sufficiently to give mankind a form of general political order without which we are all but certain to plunge into totally destructive war. The task is common to East and West, yet the West must give a lead in this matter. We have been extreme nationalists longer and therefore should by now be growing out of that painful malady, whereas the East has caught the fever of nationalism only recently and is in a more virulent stage of the disease. We who should be getting more immune to the old ideas are, therefore, the only group from which a lead can come in constructing a general order of security for mankind.

Formal constitution-drafting is not the right approach. For one thing, we are dealing with a perfectly new situation. To devise institutions for mankind as a whole—a planetary system, if you like—is very far, in its complexity and scale, from even the greatest experiment made in federation so far—that of the Founding Fathers. For another, any form of international government, being as remote as any government can be from the people it governs, runs desperate risks of being oppressive and intolerable to average human beings. Government is never very pleasant but the further it is removed the worse it can become. Obviously, anything as remote as a system of general international order must be the minimum compatible with our not blowing ourselves up. I must confess that when I think about world-planning authorities I begin to flinch. Much of the value in human life lies in its variety and richness and diversity. We do not want to ensure survival from extinction at the cost of extinguishing everything that made life worth living in the first place.

What we are looking for is, then, a minimum plan for international order, the minimum necessary to prevent atomic war with the maximum amount of variety and diversity that is possible within such a framework. The starting point must, I believe, be the nation state. Nationalism has been pushed to a lunatic extreme but nations have, none the less, a continuing and organic identity. World order, for instance, need no more abolish the nation state than the existence of a French state implies calling all Frenchmen Dubonnet. The state, as historically developed, has staying power, it has unity in diversity, it has a common loyalty. All these are very valuable things. What is wrong is that modern nationalism is like cancer in a healthy body: it has gone so far in its pretensions and claims that it threatens to destroy the whole social order. But that does not mean that the national community, like the organic cell, is not basically a healthy thing. So let us not conceive a world order in which everyone is called something like XY2Z.

Now, is there any analogy in history which we might take to guide us in moving towards a balanced world order? One might discuss the problem in terms of the United Nations since it seems the nearest institution we have to an instrument of general government. But there are two reasons for hesitating. The first is that absolute state sovereignty is still enshrined in the Charter. The second is that ten years' practical functioning is a very short time for judgment. I do not say that the United Nations might not be the embryo of world order but it does not tell us what functions the nation states have to surrender to a higher authority. For guidance on that point, we must look elsewhere.

One of the most remarkable institutions in the whole history of mankind was the old Chinese Empire. It held together a vast mass of mankind living with every kind of climate and geography and including a broad range of tribal loyalties and historical traditions. It also maintained its unity in diversity over a longer period than any other system we have known. The interesting point about the Chinese imperial structure was that it touched very few things. It defended the frontiers and dealt directly with the punishment of violence, in other words, external or internal aggression; it concerned itself with the maintenance of the very elaborate irrigation system which was necessary to ensure Chinese food supplies. It was also charged with countering disaster and famine

(111)

and undertook the control of foodstuffs in times of short-age. Thus the imperial government performed what one might call the minimum task of keeping order. It dealt with aggressive crimes. It attempted to keep some sort of over-all economic balance of stability. Within that framework, the provinces, the family, the clans, the pro-vincial organizations, the lawyers, the merchants—all enjoyed a high degree of autonomy and were strongly encouraged to settle most of their internal affairs by mediation and agreement. Here, then, is a possible anal-ogy with the kind of minimum institutions that we might employ in order to prevent ourselves from destroying life permanently on this planet. On the one hand, we must accept institutions and processes which ensure the peaceful settlement of disputes. On the other, a central authority needs some powers to ensure general economic stability.

First, then, the peaceful settlement of disputes—this may seem difficult enough if we look round the world and think of the number of disputes that are going on now. On the other hand, it is equally legitimate to look at conditions in a rather more optimistic way and re-member the areas within which nobody any longer thinks of settling disputes by force. A large part of the world today does not intend to use force. What is needed is to institutionalize that intention—to formalize means of arbitration and conciliation, and to strengthen the

Court of International Justice, and to back these institutions by some international method of using police powers if methods of peaceful conciliation are put aside by one or other of the contestants. This last point is the most difficult for nationalism to accept. Yet it is the only means of removing sanctions from the individual decision of the Powers, great or small.

Such minimum political arrangements would, of course, be greatly reinforced by the existence of functioning international economic institutions. One of the obvious ways of underpinning an international system, based on law, not force, would be to prevent conflicts and disputes from reaching such a pitch of embitteredness that they can *only* be settled by violence. Not all disputes begin in economics (very far from it), but nevertheless, certain forms of economic stress and stringency are such that nations and groups involved in them no longer behave in a rational manner. For instance, it is reasonably certain that Germany could have solved its problems without Hitler had it not been for the despair and misery caused by the 1929 depression. The disintegration of the German economy in that crisis created conditions of desperation and political extremism of which the Nazi Party was able to take advantage.

Therefore, if we are to have much hope of settling our disputes peacefully, we must have the means to make sure that conflicts do not reach an extreme point. We have to ensure that nations are not driven to violence by overpopulation, by too much pressure on resources, by inability to feed themselves, by inability to trade—by all these classical pressures which, for instance, started Japan out on its path of imperialism after the nineteen-twenties. Nor is the outlook for such action too discouraging. At least the technical and economic means are available. One of the vast changes brought about by industry, technology and science in this century is that once we abandon the purely national approach, our power to deal with extreme economic pressures is almost infinitely great. Again and again, when we say that we cannot cope with a certain economic situation, what we really mean is: "If I were to cope with it effectively, I should have to do something beyond my frontiers, which I am not prepared to do." Europe's dilemma in 1947—between rising demands and falling dollar reserves—would have been insoluble if America had not decided to act beyond its frontiers in the Marshall Plan.

There is no shortage of information on what international economic institutions are needed to reinforce the peaceful settlement of disputes. In fact, the reports that have been written on the subject within the Atlantic area since 1947 now number upwards of a dozen, and all point more or less in the same direction. The score of this particular orchestral piece has been prepared

again and again and again; the only trouble is that the
orchestra will not play. Now, if you want, as I say, to
see what kind of minimal institutions are needed in our
economic life, I would recommend the Grey Report, the
Bell Report, the Rockefeller Report, the Paley Report,
the vast documentation of the Organization for European Economic Co-operation and so many more. But
the point is that most of these studies support more or
less the same conclusion: that we need probably three
master institutions for regulating our economic life in
the international sphere. The first is an extended version
of the International Monetary Fund to deal with the
exchange and convertibility of currencies; the second is
an organization to deal with the problems of balancing
international trade at the highest and not at the lowest
level. The proposed Organization for Trade Co-operation
might be the embryo of such an agency. The third is an
organization for ensuring the movement of capital, and
possibly of population as well. Part of its functions are
already covered—although on too modest a scale—by
the World Bank for International Reconstruction and
the new International Finance Corporation. These are
minimum economic institutions which may perhaps be
said to correspond to the public works, irrigation, and
famine relief undertaken by the Chinese imperial government. They are the least onerous institutions we need
to create some form of economic stability in our world

and to prevent disputes and difficulties becoming embittered by the pressure of economic want and the envy, hate, and spite which want creates.

Let us now suppose that, by some miracle of insight and courage, we do enhance, extend, and make effective such institutions. What then? How can they be effective, for is not our world split down the middle between the Communists and the free? It is all very well to talk about functioning international organizations. It may be fun to draw up minimum blueprints (I would underline that word, *minimum*. I have tried to suggest the minimum in this field, for the maximum would be intolerable). But at the end of it all, the Communists can sabotage the whole attempt.

The first thing to be said is that over large areas of this world's surface, what the Communist will or will not do has absolutely no bearing on this problem. Nationalism is world wide; but Communism is confined, and we hope it continues to be so, to perhaps one-third of the world's surface, perhaps a bit more: too much, in fact, but still not even half the world. Within the area where the Communist writ does not run, we are co-operating under a free system of sovereign national states; and nobody is going to thwart us if we set to work in this area to make experiments in the sacrifice and pooling of sovereignty. When I look at this field of free-world sovereignty I am reminded of a lot of bathers standing round a very cold pond and constantly putting in a toe to test the temperature. They all know that at some point they have to get into that pond, and it probably will not be so bad when they do, but as long as they go on touching the problem of sovereignty with one toe, and shrinking back, how very unpleasant it seems!

Schemes like NATO, our adherence to the United Nations, plans like the Colombo Plan or the Marshall Plan, are the toes we put in to feel out the water. It seems pretty cold; and we draw back. Then come second thoughts: "Oh well, we have to get in." So back we come and feel the water with yet another Plan. But we postpone the real decision, which is to get in and say: "All right, together with all nations sufficiently like-minded to make this experiment, we will recognize that the day of unlimited national sovereignty is past. We will set up a functioning international order in a world which is now as small as the continental United States a hundred years ago." Once we have reached that point, the objection that half the world is Communist will be irrelevant, because we shall have begun to act in the areas in which we are already free to act now, if only we can make up our minds.

Incidentally, to pursue our own policies in our part of the world would also prove the best way of dealing with Communism. One of the great troubles in our present policy towards Communism is that we seem to spend our time saying: "What is Uncle Khrushchev doing? Let us go and try to prevent it." It seems to me that if we had a policy of our own for developing the kind of institutions we need for sane international living, we might experience the reverse process and find the Russians actually wanting to know what *we* were up to: frankly, since the great days of the Marshall Plan, they have not had to show a flicker of interest. They have the idea—and we encourage it—that they hold the center of the stage and everyone else will more or less dance to their tune. So, quite apart from the survival of humanity, even the short-term interest of waging the cold or cooling war would be served if we tried to establish the kind of political and economic order by which we can hope to avoid extinction. We should soon maneuver the Communists into the position of having to find out what *we* were doing, and possibly even asking if they might do it too.

A new approach of this kind is of particular importance in our relations with Asia. The first reason is political. If international relations continue to be conducted on the base of raw national interest, the chief aspect of Western policy will continue to recall all the centuries when Western nationalism was the equivalent, in Eastern minds, of imperialism and colonialism. The suspicion will persist that behind Western national interest still lies a propensity to control and exploit Eastern lands.*

The second reason concerns economics—or rather, the point where politics and economics overlap. If we were to accept seriously the aim of using international co-operation to check the world's potential disasters before they reach the explosive stage, we would find, inevitably, that much of our effort was being directed to Asia. There the hopes for capital growth and development are far more uncertain than in the West, and the pressure of population and need infinitely greater.

Moreover, Asia would be the great beneficiary if, as one of the main lines in our international policy, we were to adopt the social principle which has been of such immense service within our own communities, the principle of the wealthy helping the not-so-wealthy and the use of capital creatively to bring up conditions of living on all sides. In the first stages of our international economic co-operation, we would find that a large part of the work we had to do would consist of the wealthier Western nations undertaking a long-term co-operative

* The Anglo-French intervention at Suez, however interpreted in London and Washington, seems in Asian eyes a conclusive demonstration that colonial attitudes persist in the West. The Communists are also trying with all possible emphasis to pin the colonial tag on President Eisenhower's definition of American interest in a non-Communist Middle East. The crisis and the aftermath of Suez thus illustrate the urgency of giving as strong an international orientation as possible to Western initiatives in Asia and the need to separate, as much as may be, purely Western interests of a strategic or even economic kind from broad policies of aid and reconstruction in Eastern countries.

effort to raise the standards of Asia: and they would be doing so through international agencies—a method which would remove still further the taint of "Western exploitation." In short, a policy of international economic co-operation, based on the traditional principles of the democratic West, leads inevitably to the most effective method of defeating the Communist conspiracy in Asia and of creating, East and West together, the kind of world in which humanity may yet hope to survive.

Having said so much, one must also admit that such proposals counter the strongest, deepest, most widespread political instinct of our age—the spirit of total national sovereignty. Even when one talks about these minimum essential conditions for a functioning world order, one has the sense of being if not exactly in Cloud-Cuckoo-Land, yet of trespassing dangerously near its frontiers. If nationalism is still our strongest preoccupation, is there any force, any psychic strength, any ideal, any vision, which we can invoke to jerk ourselves out of the parochialism in which we have lived so disastrously for the last four hundred years? Is there any insight in our own civilization which can help us over this new great divide of humanity?

We may hope there is something in human momentum. It is true that the political organization of mankind has grown from the tribe to the state and the federation.

And this movement has, in the Western world, in spite of the waxing and waning of empires, followed a thread of developing freedom—from the city states in the medieval community to the constitutional nation state in Holland and Britain and then on to a free federal community as broad and wide as the United States. It may be that this expanding pattern of organized freedom need not stop short at the edge of genuine international order. But I am not a determinist. History is moved forward by men and ideas. We cannot rely upon supposed momentum. So, while admitting that at the moment nothing seems stronger than parochialism and national myopia, we must ask if there is anything else upon which we can draw to raise our sights a little, and give an international order some kind of wider backing, some greater vision and stronger ideal.

I suppose that, first of all, we can do something on the basis of fear. Fear has done a great deal for mankind. It can be the beginning of wisdom provided we fear the right things. In the past, fear has often been a good taskmaster, and today, if we think for a moment, we ought to be scared into our wits by the mushroom cloud, by all the new weapons and instruments of extinction that not only can sear our lives in this generation but may, by mutating and recessing genes, destroy any hope of normal humanity hereafter. If we are not scared of that, one wonders what we ever shall be scared of. So I think it can be argued that fear will help us, fear, taking the form of a desire for national survival.

On the other hand, national survival alone is probably not enough. It still draws its strength from the idea of exclusive nationhood, and it is, in part, this concentration, this obsession with nationhood that has brought us to our present dilemma. So we must ask whether mankind has any vision that transcends frontiers; are men irretrievably tribal animals? Or can some wider ideal or hope or ambition help them to leave the parochial gods behind?

One approach to this problem could lie in looking at the answers which over the generations men themselves have given to the question of what manner of men they are. And perhaps the starting point is the fact that the questions have in fact been asked. Curiosity, clearly, is one of the first marks of the human race. Once man awoke from the animal beatitude of having neither past nor future, and of not knowing he was going to die, he began to ask questions. He knows that his life is transient, he witnesses death and destruction, he is conscious deeply in himself of being not self-sufficient but wholly dependent upon things that he does not understand. Thus, from the beginning, in our most primitive religions, there is combined a sense of trying to placate what cannot be understood and an attempt to reach out for explanations, manipulations, and controls. Homo sapiens should perhaps be homo curiosus—I think the sapience and the curiosity began together.

Parenthetically, one of the remarkable points about our own Western civilization is that, although all civilizations and systems of thought have attempted some explanation of man's estate, none has asked the questions so doggedly and unassuageably as our Western society. In fact, it sometimes seems that the sign of our civilization should be a question mark. At our Jewish roots, we find the book of Job, in which Job, unlike most of the early philosophers of mankind, did most vigorously question the ways of God with man. The answer he received was, in some ways, inconclusive, but the fascinating thing in the whole Book of Job is the almost modern tone of doubt, of anxiety, of agony, of passion to know the answer. Then again, it was our Greek forebears who developed the Socratic method, of pursuing the truth, from question to question, eliminating the contradictory and illogical, and following the clue of reason as though curiosity were a bloodhound seeking truth in its lair. The medieval schoolmen, for all the strictness of the framework within which they worked, practiced disputation, debate, and logical analysis with a rigor that made them, as Professor Whitehead suggested, forerunners of the scientific inquirers in later centuries.

And as the modern age dawned, it found its archetype

in Faust, the man who questioned everything—every temporal thing, every heavenly thing—and finally found salvation—a forerunner, here, of our twentieth-century "salvation by public works"—by helping, in a selfless moment, to drain a marsh and aid his fellow men.

I do not think we shall ever still this questioning spirit in man, particularly in men as strongly marked as modern man by the influence of Western thought. And in all the questions he proposes, there is, surely, one question which lies behind all the others and is perhaps the unquiet root from which all other questions grow. That question is: Why is man here at all? What is the purpose of this whole vast panorama of human, physical, terrestrial and planetary events in which he is plunged, yet wakes to self-consciousness with intimations of infinity and the agonizing knowledge of death?

There have, of course, been an unlimited number of answers to the riddle of man's being, but they tend to belong, one way or another, to three broad directions of thought. The first answer is one which appears widespread but which very few people accept in fact. This is the old answer of fatalism, the answer that we do not know, and that the whole thing is very largely meaningless. One of the products of ancient thought was the conviction that man's whole existence is bound to a fixed, revolving system in which all is predetermined and all recurs. Greek thought envisaged a Great Year which brought the cycle of centuries full-circle. Buddhism saw man bound to a "melancholy wheel" driven by his own desires. In the midst of this conditioned cycle of recurrence, individual life is no more than a flash of consciousness playing on a vast and meaningless pageant of unending revolving change.

In a sense, Communism harks back to that kind of fatalism. Calling fate by any other name does not change the nature of fatalism. You may call your stern goddess "dialectical materialism"; nevertheless she remains a goddess of ineluctable destiny, from whose path you cannot swerve and who controls the whole development of history according to iron law. Man, himself, is no more than a product of this process, and has no further significance.

This, philosophically speaking, is the position that the Marxist ought to take, because there is no room in the strict theory of economic determinism for human freedom, for any sort of independent action on the part of man. Nor, unless he adds the quite unprovable belief that private property is the source of all evil—is "original sin," in fact—can the Marxist explain why at the end of all the conditioned economic change, a Utopia—the classless society—should put an end to history. Ancient thinkers introduced no such gimmick; they thought that the revolving universe would go on being "nasty, brutish, and short." They did not expect a happy ending. But the Communists have lived too near to the Christian hope of resurrection and of all things made new. They have been too deeply imbued with the doctrine of progress to be content with the idea of a determined revolution according to economic law. And so, at whatever cost to logic, at the end, there is a happy outcome. The Marxist is one more proof that fatalism, as an answer to the human mystery, is losing strength. Fatalism assumes a sort of deeply ingrained pessimism about mankind which two thousand years of Christian optimism have tended to banish. Even Marxism, the most developed and systematic theory of fatalism current, borrows a happy denouement from Christian hope. As Dr. Johnson once said of Oliver Edwards's philosophy, cheerfulness will keep breaking in. There may be no logical foundation for it, nevertheless, there it is.

Marxism, in spite of its philosophical presuppositions, really belongs to a quite different approach—not of fatalism but of humanistic materialism. This is a second possibility, that man himself is the explanation of it all, and that man in his grandeur and servitude, man in his growth and development, man as a sentient animal in a material universe is his own answer and justification. Humanity itself is an object for sufficient worship. The development of the human race is enough to give meaning to the vast processions of nature by which it is surrounded. This is, in many ways, a noble view, and it is certainly one that has been fostered with great strength in the West, where man by the use of his rational faculties, by his imagination, his energy, and his creativeness, has transformed the face of the earth. Its supporters claim that it embraces all humanity and that it is a possible moral basis for a worldwide order. The service of man transcends all barriers and frontiers. Here is the ideal for which we seek.

Yet I think, for all the noble lives and actions that this religion of humanity has inspired, that it is not enough to lead us to transcend our present nationalist inhibitions. Nor do I think it gives full rein to the potential creativeness and vision of mankind.

The first limiting factor in choosing man as the meaning and center of the universe is, alas, to consider oneself. Each man, if he stops to consider, is aware of his total dependence upon a million things beyond his control simply for the daily business of living. When they fail —as fail they will—dependence turns to death. Nor is it simply a question of physical limitations. We are as aware of mental limitations and heaven knows most of us are painfully aware of moral limitations—of a will so weak and a moral purpose so feeble that we hardly keep troth or faith or pursue, even over a few weeks, any consistent line of conduct. Not even the wisest and best escape discouragement when they look at their wavering line of moral endeavor.

Because of this sense of inadequacy, there are, it seems

to me, very few people who have made gods of them-selves—the result is a disaster if they do. When people turn to a religion of mankind, they are nearly always thinking of something beyond themselves, of humanity in its collective aspect. But since humanity at large is a very amorphous concept, the worship of humanity tends to become something more precise. Lip-service may be paid to a wider ideal. But practical, effective service is rendered to the organized units of humanity—to dynasty, to empire, to nation, to class. And these ideals have in them dangerous possibilities of perversion. History shows that when politics take on a religious color—for to seek the meaning of life in a collective organization is to give it religious significance—citizens look for a godlike man to guide them, rather than to committees, assemblies or "collective leadership." The French Revolution begins with the religion of humanity and ends with Napoleon. Stalin twisted world Communism into Great Russian dictatorship. Yet no mortal man can bear the full weight of his fellows' adoration. When all the freight of human questioning, longing, and despair is shifted onto the shoulders of one man, the more likely consequence is that he will run mad—mad as we have seen them in our own day, Hitler in his bunker, Stalin dying among the terrors of his "doctors' plot." Human nature cannot bear the loneliness and the stress. Horrors of destructiveness and mania have marked the paths of dictators throughout history. And when we blame them, we should perhaps remember the weight with which they have been loaded by the communities they led. They may have started in pride and ambition. They end in a psychological wilderness, carrying the burden of the whole community, scapegoats as well as leaders. In this sense, clearly, men are not born to be their own gods.

There is another sense in which the collective image of man can lead to disaster. Our ideal may be the nation. Or we can express our wider striving in terms of the class to which we belong. But often we find that what we have produced is not a wider vision or a greater ideal, but an organization in the name of which we will commit crimes and atrocities which, in our private capacity, we would not even contemplate. When man makes a religion of his collective self, there is almost no horror that he will not commit in that name. In fact, this capacity to behave worse in one's collective capacity can even be observed—most tragically—when men establish religious communities. By giving themselves to the collective whole, some men, instead of using greater vision and wider humanity, have actually fallen to lower, more vicious and more brutal standards than would have been tolerated for a moment in private life. It is not only in the name of liberty that high-minded crime has been committed. Every collective ideal has exacted its martyrs and its blood.

In spite of the fact that religion that looks no further than humanity has inspired good men and has produced noble thought and great progress, I think the long record of history suggests that when man seeks to make a religion at the human level he tends to make a religion of his collective self, himself understood as power, as organization, and as force; his religion does not then urge him to higher levels; on the contrary, the danger is that he will drop even below the human standards which he would accept as an ordinary human being. These are not abstract historical reflections. In our own day, Communism has both caught the loyalty of sincerely convinced lovers of humanity and committed inhuman cruelties in their name.

We are then left with a third possible answer to the riddle of human life. It is the answer which, in history, man has given over the longest span and the widest space. It is the answer which, until recently, we gave in the Western world. It is that man is a being created by a benevolent and omniscient Power and that the meaning of the universe is to be unraveled in the relationship between God and man. As far as our own society is concerned, many of the institutions under which we live, many of the guiding ideas and many great visions by which we are still inspired, are derived from the day when the idea of a divine order of reality was still a living truth in the minds of most people.

Many of the most characteristic features of our civilization spring from our dynamic, history-conscious Christian tradition. The separation of divine and secular, of church and state, of the things that are God's and the things that are Caesar's has helped to create a pluralist society in which subordinate groups and corporations enjoy their own appropriate rights. The notion of a moral law transcending kings and princes (one recalls Bracton's dictum that the King was under God and the law) is another strong strand in our constitutional practice of government. Freedom has its roots in the concept of each human soul enjoying infinite value in the sight of God and bearing the grandeur and servitude of personal choice and responsibility. And if all men are children of a common Father, they are brothers at the metaphysical roots of their being. Christianity has often betrayed but never denied the brotherhood of man.

And, unique among world religions, Christianity, inheriting the vision from its Jewish roots, has seen the whole of history not as meaningless repetition but as the unfolding of the drama of God's purpose for man—a drama in which man, as free agent, has a creative part to play, transforming himself and his environment into a better, higher reflection of an ideal order. The fatalisms of antiquity gave ground before the new vision of personal and historical progress.

But if our religious tradition helped to bring our political and social order into being and nourished its growth, it certainly cannot be said to exercise any such influence today. Liberal, humane society in the West has not entirely abandoned its metaphysical beliefs. But the institutions of liberal society have been transplanted to Asia with no links to any great religious tradition. The danger facing West and East is twofold. It may be (we cannot yet be sure) that the institutions of freedom need metaphysical faith to sustain them. For instance, if you cut the painter between man and the infinite, his precious value as a soul of infinite worth may be lost. Infinite value is not something that either science or observation predicate of individual human beings. It is an act of faith and the faith may fade when man is no longer believed to contain a spark of the divine. One cannot be dogmatic. Free institutions may, indeed, enjoy a momentum of their own, but we do know that they are the exception in human affairs and have arisen only in the religions and classical tradition of the West.

The second danger is that if all answer to man's deepest questioning—What manner of man am I?—disappears from free society, other answers will come crowding in. Men will not live without their gods and one reason for Communism's sweeping success seems to lie in its ability, for a time at least, to provide a total explanation of the human predicament.

At this point a critic has every right to interrupt with impatience. Why, he might ask, do you suggest that religious faith can contribute something to the building of a worldwide international order when, on your own showing, it hardly influences the political outlook of our present divided world? Moreover, is not all this concern whether or not free institutions can survive without metaphysical faith really begging the question? Faith has faded because people no longer believe in a divine order of reality. They think the ancient religion a myth. Do you want to suggest that the rights of the individual, the principles of free government, and the building of a humane international order are to be based upon mythologies men have outgrown? Is it not precisely our greater knowledge in the last hundred years in the West of the variety of myth and legend to be found in the religions of mankind that has taught us to see them all not as a statement of everlasting truth but as projections of the wish-fulfillments and stresses of human beings who have not learnt to be content with man's estate and who have not yet mastered scientific controls of their natural environment? Is this the time to invoke religion as an inspiration for world order? Is it not in fact our knowledge of the wider world that has exploded our own parochial religious ideas?

These are serious criticisms, but I would like to suggest an opposite conclusion and to argue that on the contrary it is only now, in the new, wider and more sympathetic confrontation of Eastern and Western thought, that we can realize how our religious insights, far from being parochial, are of the very stuff of universal faith. A century ago, Western study of Eastern thought tended to be narrow and arrogant. There had been great exceptions. In the sixteenth, seventeenth, and eighteenth centuries, both in India and China, missionaries, above all, Jesuit missionaries, attempted to study Eastern religion, as it were, in depth, and such remarkable men as Father Ricci or Father Adam von Schall believed that Christian revelation could be conveyed to the Chinese by way of the Confucian ethical tradition. But in the early nineteenth century, Western study lost these deeper sympathies and Eastern religion came to be regarded as idol worship and superstition.

This attitude was followed in the West by the rationalist approach that brought all religion under the heading of superstition and argued, from the diversity of beliefs and practices, that all must be illusion. There could be no empirical or rational argument for religion, it was felt, because examination of the record showed that man's witness to religion was completely variable and contradictory.

But with the steady improvement in the depth and

seriousness of Oriental studies, I believe we have reached a new point in this century. We find that when the religions and philosophies of the East are studied more sympathetically and profoundly and compared with our own religious traditions, we are confronted not by daunting variety but by great and illuminating similarities. The basic insights into the nature of the universe which have been held by divers men in divers places and under conditions of geography and history which could hardly be more remote from each other have so much in common that they amount to what philosophers have sometimes called "the perennial philosophy." Men, in their deepest wisdom and insight, far from coming to different concepts of the nature of the universe and the purpose of life, have reached a common base of doctrine. This common philosophy was first evolved in two millennia before Christ and may well have been the greatest revolution so far in human history. Since then, it has been enriched and varied by many new insights. Yet the basic doctrines remain unchanged. God is accepted as the source of being, law, and light, and as an active power of love and compassion. The emphasis may vary. In China and in Hinayanan Buddhism you will find more weight attached to law—the way of Heaven, the Darma; and in Christianity and in Mahayanan Buddhism the emphasis is on love and compassion. For all, God is the first principle of being, the ground and substance of all existence.

The next insight that great religions seem to have in common is that each human soul has access to the law, light, and being of God because the human spirit is in some way based or grounded in the Godhead: we cannot in our limited human way describe what that link can be. It has been called by various names. The Hindus say: "That art thou." The Quakers speak of "the inner light," Catholic theologians of "the point of the soul." But the spark of divinity is in every human soul. From it the greatness, the creativeness, the unboundedness of the human spirit is derived.

The third insight upon which all are agreed is the manner in which that spark can be released to become a fire to consume the earth. It is by ending the narrow egoisms, the greeds, the angers, the envies, the hatreds —all the restricting appetites and passions which keep the individual locked up inside his mortal self. If you look at the law of life—or rather, the law of love—laid down by all the great religions, it is finally based upon a rule which the fathers of the Church have called "detachment"—a rule which enjoins sufficient objectivity toward one's own needs and sufficient compassion toward the needs of others to let the self break out of the closed circle of egoism. Then each man can meet his neighbor with love—in other words, with an active intention to secure his good. He can see his friend and neighbor in all who come to him. He can even envisage the unity of all human beings in one neighborhood or family—"the family of man."

I would therefore say that, on any empirical basis, insights of this depth appearing in cultures so different and conditions so diverse do suggest that at the deepest level of human wisdom there is a unity of vision embracing all mankind; more, that this vision is compatible with humane and liberal institutions, indeed, demands them, since compulsion and dictatorship deny the free spirit of man and cramp his capacity for love. It is in fear-ridden societies that neighborliness ceases to be. It would, indeed, be tempting at this point to round off this discussion with a hopeful forecast of idealism restored by closer knowledge of the world's great religions and faith in the fatherhood of God and the brotherhood of man providing a new emotional stimulus to the task of creating the institutions we need to live peacefully together, East and West, Asia and Atlantic community within the world's shrinking frontiers. Such a vision might make an excellent peroration. Unfortunately, it would not fit the facts.

It may be that the erosion of religion in the West by rationalism and materialism has come to a halt at midcentury. Certainly, the *avant garde* today is no longer Marxist. "Mysticism" is no longer equated with nonsense. The questions asked by younger people, if not specifically religious, invite a religious answer.* We may not, therefore, be too wide of the mark in believing that a revived interest in religion may be in the making in the West. It is also possible that this revival may be strengthened by greater knowledge of Eastern religious tradition in which the sense of divine transcendence and of the possibility of mystical experience have been preserved in great purity during recent centuries when, in the West, religion tended to be expressed in practical, almost utilitarian form. But the fact that should check any facile optimism is that the rational and materialist revolution in thinking which has harrowed the West since the eighteenth century is now spreading to the East, acting as it did in Europe as a dissolvent of old faiths, and as generator first of doubt and skepticism and later of new dogmatic faiths intolerant of all but supposedly "scientific" formulae.

The kind of thought which has disintegrated traditional religion in Europe will disintegrate traditional religion in the East, and it will disintegrate it all the faster in that in many places in the East the more philosophical, the more rational, and, indeed, the more elevated forms of religion have always been threatened and encroached on by mythological, superstitious, even animist types of religion. In India, although in the highest

* A remarkable recent book, *The Outsider,* by Colin Wilson (Boston, Houghton Mifflin, 1956), illustrates the metaphysical preoccupations of a new generation.

reaches of philosophy religious insights maintain unique
levels of purity and contemplation, at the village level,
among the popular religions, you are back in the realm
of mythology which, under the dissolvent of modern
thought, will prove as impossible to maintain as, say,
a belief in the Greek gods in a modern Western community. In China, the Confucian ethic which, as a mir-
ror of the Natural Law, so attracted the Jesuit Missionaries, was dominant mainly among the governing class.
Popular Taoist and Buddhist religion was legendary
and mythological. In any case, all the old orthodoxies
of China are now under attack from the new orthodoxy
of Communism, itself a bastard of Western rationalism.

When, therefore, people talk about the confrontation
of East and West and the enrichment of our religious
life by Eastern experience, they sometimes forget that
the East has yet to face the disintegrating energies of
Western scientific and materialist thought, and that
when the full impact is felt, as it is beginning to be
felt in China, it may well be that less will be left of
religious attitudes in the East than is left in Europe now.
It follows that the task of our Western world in helping
to create a tolerable humane world order is not exhausted
when a Western lead has been given away from exclusive
sovereignty or when Western abundance has been set
to work to relieve Eastern need. There remains a further
obligation—to draw upon Western religious experience

in what one might call this postrationalist age and discover whether any developments in our thinking can help to prevent the extinction in the East of all save the fierce, rationalist, obsessively dogmatic secular faiths which threaten to sweep the Orient today.

You will not expect me to give more than a hint of how such a program could be fulfilled. It would be the task of church leaders, of universities, of scholarly institutions of all kinds, of thoughtful men and women in many different professions and walks of life to attempt this confrontation of the deepest philosophical and metaphysical concepts of East and West. Some part of their work would undoubtedly lie in clarifying the profound elements of unity and common insight of which we have already spoken. On the Western side, however, we would have to offer our special experience of living through the centuries of rationalist criticism and materialist attack. And I personally believe that some of the most cogent arguments for the religious view of man and his destiny will be found to lie precisely at the point where modern thinking is supposed and indeed proclaimed to be most at odds with the religious approach. "Science" is the catch-cry of the Communists, the sole "objective" science of politics, the sole "scientific" method of liberating man from superstition and ignorance. Yet, after the first intoxication of results gained by manipulating matter and after the clearing away on the religious side of much superstition and prejudice, deeper thought has shown us in the West that there need be no essential conflict between science and religion as was so fiercely assumed in Victorian times. The Communists' continued addiction to the idea is incidentally one more evidence of their inability to move mentally into a new century.

For instance, the witness of science that the universe is orderly can hardly be said to contradict religion. The Greeks, who believed harmony to be an attribute of the Godhead, would certainly not have felt that there was anything opposed to the idea of a Primal Lawgiver in the fact that the universe in fact obeys laws. The concept of a rational First Cause is not contradicted by any amount of demonstration of proximate causes.

But, of course, the gods which science banishes are the poetic, mythological figures, not the austere Ground of Being. Yet, even here, I feel that the picture of the universe given by modern science need not contradict the religious imagination—Einstein's "sense of wonder" without which neither science nor religion can exist. We shall no longer personify the forces of nature and express our awe by imagining a thundering Zeus, or picturing the vast movements of natural energy in gods of life and death such as Vishnu and Siva. Yet the religious imagination of awe and humility might well be rekindled when we discover, by way of our atomic sciences, that the universe, far from being a tidy, Victorian place

(141)

of orderly atoms, waiting to be manipulated for man's convenience, is a vast, rushing place of energy, in which everywhere we stand, everything we touch, everything we even sit on, is a confluence of force, pouring onward, apparently, in unending creation. The very vastness, the very limitlessness of space and time, as they are now revealed, seem far more in keeping with what we might imagine to be the work of an omnipotent Creator than the old limited idea of Creation occurring some 6000 years ago on a precise date.

But perhaps the most striking way in which scientific discovery and theory can be shown to be compatible with the deepest insights of religion is to be seen in an area in which, more than any other, old faiths have dissolved and new antireligious dogmatism has arisen. The processes of evolution whereby man has developed from remote ages and the most primitive biological forms to his present sentience and self-consciousness have shaken millions in their faith in man as a spiritual being, created in the image of God. Perhaps more than any other thing, it has shaken belief in the two orders, sacred and profane, and has thrust man down into the closed order of material conditioning. Backed by cumulative scientific evidence, this account of man's origins will sweep away the mythological explanations still current in Asia. And in so far as Communism represents itself, by pseudo-scientific arguments, as the end of that process, it can make the fading of the old beliefs serve its Utopian vision.

Yet Western religion—Christianity with its roots in Judaism—has always taught a progressive unfolding of man's destiny. May it not be that the supposed conflict with the scientific picture of millennial evolution is a conflict of terms and imagination rather than of essential fact? We know the long process by which we have come to be, from the amoeba, on through forms of animal life, up to sentience and finally to self-conscious being. Now I cannot for the life of me think why it should be thought scientific to imagine that a process that has been going on through millennia has stopped in the twentieth century. By any rational judgment, we are in the middle of a still-continuing process. The profound, the vital question is to know the direction in which we are still to go.

On the evidence, we can say that evolution has brought life upwards from formless matter to full humanity by way of higher and higher levels of consciousness, freedom, and creativeness. The direction has been from the conditioned to the less conditioned, from the biologically fixed to the mentally free. It seems therefore rationally likely that the next phase of our development depends not upon material change but upon mind, will, creativeness—the highest growing points of contemporary life.

In other words, the Jewish vision of a divine drama

unfolding in time and the cosmic Christian vision of a new humanity coming to birth after millennia of bondage—which on its first formulation struck across every archaic conception of creation bound to a revolving wheel of change—has in this latter time been shown to be profoundly, imaginatively, and prophetically in tune with man's scientific discoveries of his origins.

And, in spite of the false claims of Utopian Communism which now seeks to capture the imagination of the East, we can say with rational conviction that if progress hitherto has advanced from the conditioned to the unconditioned, from the biologically bound to the mentally and creatively free, the likelihood of man's future advance lying with societies which stifle his freedom and compel him to believe in material conditioning is contradicted by the whole evidence of his millennial past.

On the contrary, if we look around us for growing points of consciousness, creativeness, and new life, we do not find them among the conquerors and dictators; we do not find them among the commissars and bureaucrats. We find them, in fact, where, remembering that frail man has flourished and the dinosaurs are extinct, we might expect to find them—among the philosophers, the sages, and the saints.

It seems to me that the Eastern idea that the highest aim of man is to achieve unity with a higher consciousness, to move to new levels of freedom by breaking away from the constraining egoisms of the self, can, at this point, be fruitfully confronted with the great Christian doctrine of the second Adam—the doctrine that Christ is the first-born of a new race of men. Here surely we have a clue to our future more convincing than the pretensions of tyrants or the greeds of classes or the aggressions of national groups. They indeed have the deadly repetitiveness of the "melancholy wheel." But if what we seek is a new type of life, which expands human consciousness, takes man beyond his present level of intelligence, and raises him to new heights of creativeness and capacity, we have to look for it in the great leaders of the world's religions, and, above all, in Christ himself.

In other words, this religious insight is not mythology: it is something so deeply embedded in human nature, so deeply rooted in human history that I think we can confidently say that whatever the setbacks, whatever the material pressures, whatever the temporary triumphs of false beliefs and false hopes, the drive of history lies in that direction and in it we are all called to play a part. If we can keep this faith, God willing, we shall be able to help our Eastern brothers when they go through the darkness of doubt, when they too are engulfed in technology and materialism, when they forget the divine image in which they are made and believe that the purpose of science is not to make truth manifest but to make gadgets. That day will come and perhaps we can be prepared for it, because it is a dark valley through which we have gone, and out of which perhaps we are beginning to emerge. Having made the biggest of all gadgets —which is the hydrogen bomb—we may have come to the conclusion that what is vital is not our material gadgets but the purpose of life which they may or may not help us to fulfill. And in rediscovering the purpose of life, we may be able, East and West together, to discover the moral unity without which political and economic unity will only be built on sand.

This may seem a tall order. But, then, humanity is a very tall order and always has been. And if our task were simple, it would not be adequate. If our faith were easy, it would not be true.

Epilogue

SOME YEARS HAVE PASSED since the lectures on which this book is based were given in Montreal. Yet the passage of time has not altered the facts or relationships which they tried to disentangle. Nothing needs to be subtracted. But something should be added—an extra dimension of crisis and urgency to every former diagnosis that was suggested or remedy that was proposed. In the last half-decade, nothing has stood still. The choice between planetary destruction or a wholly new ordering of our way of life has become steadily more inescapable. Human misery is in a period of such spate, with such turbulent forces driving it forward, that its energies will engulf us unless we can canalize them for human use. If we could do so, the revolution launched two centuries ago by the philosophers, the scientists, and the entrepreneurs of the West might still build "a new heaven or a new earth." Unchecked, it threatens a new deluge.

The starting point of our thinking about the world has to be this revolution. It conditions us all—East and West, Communist and non-Communist, rich or poor. The application of science and technology to the whole range of human activities involves mankind in processes of violent change unlike anything it has experienced before and confronts it with a fact hitherto unknown in human history—the fact of abundance. When the hunters and the food-gatherers began to give way before settled agriculture and the growth of cities—our only comparable revolution—the transformation took place over millennia. Even though it introduced entirely new ways of thinking and working, it did so in a manner that was "vaster than empires and more slow." But Western sailors and merchants, bursting into the Indian Ocean as the fifteenth century came to a close, were heralds of a total and accelerating revolution in humanity's affairs which has remained unfinished since.

Today the revolution is dominated by two facts. The first is that since the revolution began in northern Europe, making use of the coal and iron ore with which the Northern land mass is so amply provided, most of the technological development of our world society has occurred to the North of the Tropic of Cancer, and it is here that the staggering fact of abundance is beginning to be faced. If one considers the revolution of scientific change as a single process steadily involving all mankind, one can say that, broadly speaking, all the men of the Northern Hemisphere are in the van of the human column while the Southern regions bring up the rear. All are on the march but the North is ahead. As a result, it is wealthy and growing wealthier. The rearguard is actually losing ground and will continue to do so until the revolution of science and capital is completed in the Southern lands.

The second fact cuts across this North-South division. It is that the North has evolved two methods of transformation—the pragmatic, experimental, plural methods of what we can best call "the mixed economy," and the centralized, monolithic pattern of Communist planning. The Southern regions are thus offered a choice of method, and to the attractions of Communism for the developing lands already mentioned in these pages, one should add the fact that Communism as a technique of rapid economic expansion was first tried out in what was essentially an "underdeveloped area."

In Czarist Russia, Western capitalism had set the processes of change in motion. Railways had been built, and export crops had been stimulated to serve Western markets. There were some small beginnings of industry. A small elite had acquired some Westernized education. But the traditional autocratic rule of the Czars lay heavily across the vast land; and out in the countryside, where seventy per cent of the people still lived, the peasants practiced forms of static agriculture unchanged for generations, and country gentlemen lived on their rents.

We do not know whether from these incoherent and patchy beginnings, a full modernized apparatus in industry and farming could have developed. As it stood, Russian society was essentially unstable—the new modern sector was big enough to rouse aspirations but not big enough to satisfy them. Society was desperately insecure even before the outbreak of war in 1914. The four-year conflict delivered the *coup de grâce*.

Chaos gave a small body of dedicated Bolsheviks the chance to seize power and a decade later, after much confusion and many false starts, to apply to the task of modernizing the economy the methods of total state planning and total mobilization of capital which the Western Powers had evolved after 1916 in their efforts to win the first World War. Brutal as the methods were, they gave Russia a structure of heavy industry strong enough to withstand Hitler and broad enough to carry the country from the wooden plough to the space satellite in forty years.

Most of the lands to the south of the Tropic of Cancer have emerged from their first encounters with Western capitalism in much the same condition as Czarist Russia in 1914. In India and China—the two lands of destiny in Asia—we find the same consequence of partial modernization—some infrastructure, particularly in transport, some export crops, the beginning of industry and of Western education, but an unchanged and—in Asia —increasingly bankrupt countryside. Society as a result lacked both cohesion and momentum. Since China, too, underwent a fifty-year nightmare of internal war and external invasion, it is not surprising that there, as in Russia, in 1917, a determined and dedicated Communist minority could take over power and begin the experiment of total economic mobilization. India, which had enjoyed over a century of internal peace under a stable administration and mercifully missed the horrors of a Japanese occupation, opted for milder, more pragmatic and more liberal methods of modernization. One can only underline the point already made on earlier pages that, with this decision, a drama of comparative choice opened in Asia which must affect profoundly the rest of the developing world.

The issue is not decided. After a decade of planning in both countries, it is still difficult to be dogmatic about anything, least of all about Chinese claims and statistics. One can cautiously hazard the guess that since China seems to have saved a much larger proportion of its national income—over twenty per cent compared with not much more so far than ten per cent in India—the base of its economy is growing more rapidly. Transport, power, coal, steel—the keys to expansion—have all grown at a quicker pace than in India. Between 1958 and 1960, for instance, the Chinese claimed to have increased their output of steel from eight million tons to eighteen million tons. The quality of much of this—particularly the so-called "backyard steel"—may be pretty dubious, but the Indian figure for 1960 was still under three million tons.

In agriculture, one must confess to the same uncertainty. China seems to be following the Russian technique of dealing out to its peasants an alternating treatment of kicks and encouragement. When, in 1958, the total communization of the land was announced, the "Communes" were hailed as the first stage of Communism—thus putting China ideologically ahead of Russia. But in 1960 to 1961, after a combination of disastrous floods and droughts and an apparent increase in peasant discontent and exhaustion, the communes were considerably modified and some private rights restored to the villages. Meanwhile China—with its population increasing by twelve million a year—has been buying massive supplies of grain abroad. Just as in the Soviet Union, where farming has lagged far behind progress in other sectors, it may be that in China, too, communal agriculture and all unwilling peasants will be a dangerous drag on the whole country's prospects of growth.

Yet India's gentler revolution of change has not yet proved itself either. It has become a commonplace of development policy to say that general modernization cannot succeed unless the agricultural sector is shaken out of the rut of subsistence farming. Otherwise the countryside cannot produce the food the cities need, provide savings for the transference to new sectors of the economy, or become a lively market for the new products of industry. But to argue that traditional farming must be changed is easier than to do it. A decade of

Community Development in India and Pakistan has given remarkably uneven results. In some areas, where farmers are keen and farming traditions progressive, the village economy has been transformed. In others, Community Development has passed almost without trace over the surface of village life, leaving perhaps only a community hall permanently locked to show for all its labors. Food production has increased but only just enough to keep ahead of the population. A genuinely dynamic agriculture has still to be achieved.

Yet the ten years have not been wasted. Out of the experiments and failures and confusions has come a growing conviction that if the same administrative skills, careful planning, and capital investment are applied to areas of agricultural development as are normally mobilized for, say, large-scale public works, a breakthrough to better farming can be achieved. So, in both India and Pakistan, the new pattern of community development turns on choosing a "project area" or devoting to it in a concentrated form all available skills, resources and techniques—fertilizers, better seeds, water, feeder roads, cooperative credit and advice, and, if possible, a master plan of land use for the region. This new approach, if successful, has significance far beyond Asia.

Africa and Latin America have to make their way out of the closed circuit of stagnant agriculture. Cooperative institutions, new skills, and generous capital properly combined may show the way.

Admittedly, the program remains one of extreme difficulty, and farm output has to go up fast enough to make savings available for both the farms and the cities. But without savings, can output go up? This is the vicious circle in which so much of the world's farming is still caught. The circle can be broken by the provision of capital from other sources. It was European capital, moving out massively to other temperate lands in the nineteenth century that created new dynamic systems of agriculture—in North America, in Australasia, in Argentina. But today is such capital likely to be forthcoming on a sufficient scale? The Atlantic area actually faces a glut of food. Its demands on other continents have not grown in proportion to its own growth since more advanced technology and the invention of substitutes—in fibres, in chemicals—have lessened its need to look outside its own wealthy frontiers. The old "natural" transfusion of growth from developed to underdeveloped areas by way of investment and trade has slackened. Market forces, left to themselves, would not counter but would actually increase the gap between the rich nations of the North and the poor emergent lands to the South. Can the essential transfer, then, be accomplished by other means, for instance, by a planned policy of trade and aid? At this point, however, we leave the dilemmas of the developing world and enter another realm of politics—the decision and vision of the Atlantic community.

Clearly the kind of sustained policies Western nations are likely to follow depend fundamentally on their view of our revolutionary world. If we see ourselves as living in a separate universe of sovereign states with very limited resources and no lasting obligations beyond our frontiers, we can rationally decide that the increasing misery of a third of the human race is no concern of ours. We can "pass by on the other side." If, however, our wealth has grown out of all recognition, if our destiny is enmeshed at every point in the single web of humanity, if the limit of our concern is in fact the entire human race dwelling on this narrow planet, then the needs and aspirations of the millions less fortunate than ourselves must be our inescapable obligation, our task and our destiny for so long as any of us can look ahead. This is the fundamental decision which will determine all other decisions—are we or are we not trying to create a world order in which all men can live and work and prosper together?

The arguments for world order are, of course, as inescapable as the hydrogen bomb. Science and technology have abolished space, created instant worldwide communication, unleashed unimaginable resources, and exposed the whole human race to the possibility of nuclear destruction. The last half-decade has not minimized these facts. On the contrary, the inescapable interweaving of human destiny has grown closer as the jets banish the miles between continents and Mr. Khrushchev explodes his fifty-megaton bomb. To transform this fearful solidarity of potential extinction into a fruitful moral solidarity governed by law and mutual trust is now more than ever man's fundamental task.

And, one might say with justification, the task seems now more than ever impossible. The cold war hovers on the edge of hot war, tempers are more exasperated, positions more rigid, fears more aroused than ever before. How can one speak, in the middle of ideological deadlock and hostility, of an effort to give international society the essential minimum institutions of a common life—the rule of law, peaceful settlements of disputes, economic organs of cooperation and welfare? The list of needs may not have changed in the last six years. But surely the possibility of attaining them has grown bleaker still.

Yet the free world has not lost its ability to make a

creative start. The Thirteen Colonies were the nucleus of an American federation, Piedmont the catalyst of a free Italy. International order of an organic kind created in one part of the planet could await the day when its experiment and example could be adopted more widely. Nothing save their own will stands in the way of the Atlantic Powers should they seek to make the effort. And at this point we confront the encouraging fact that the last half-decade has brought astonishing and creative changes. Western Europe's Common Market, fusing the economies of France, Federal Germany, Italy, and the Low Countries has proved so phenomenally successful that Britain, and most of the remaining states in free Europe, seek to join. At the same time, the idea of the Common Market has become a symbol of closer cooperation within the developing continents—in Latin America, in Africa, in Southeast Asia. And such moves could be encouraged and fostered if present trends in Western economic aid also proved permanent.

After a decade of somewhat haphazard giving, the American administration is trying to introduce three new coordinating principles into the operation of its programs of assistance: the first that aid should be longterm and sustained; the second that all wealthy Western nations should play their part, by contributing possibly an agreed percentage of their national income; the third that recipient nations should prepare careful plans of development into which foreign assistance can be fitted rationally and without waste. In fact, India has become a central factor in this new approach since a Western consortium of the major Atlantic Powers under the chairmanship of the World Bank negotiates the scale and pattern of external aid and coordinates with India its role in India's own plans for growth. Under this new system, it seems likely that the Indians will receive from all Western sources—with some additions from the Soviet bloc—something like a billion dollars a year in external capital and a sizable part of it in very longterm, low-interest-rate development loans. The chief element of uncertainty in the duel between India and China—availability of capital—may thus be on the way to being resolved.

These are startling advances towards the type of mutual support and cooperation our nascent world society most urgently needs. If it is developed and formalized—for instance, by a North American association with the Common Market inside an Atlantic Community, by the full acceptance of the principle that longterm aid should be a permanent lien on the wealthy nations' resources, by the extension of cooperation to the involved and inflamed issues of international trade—then it would be possible without too much Utopianism to see an Atlantic Community, growing steadily in coherence and prosperity, using its capital and its commerce to encourage growth in other Common Markets—in South America, in Asia, in Africa—and at some point forming with them a kind of federation of federations which would give two-thirds of the world a loose but functioning framework of international order.

Nor would we doubt that such a strengthening of the non-Communist world would profoundly affect its relations with the Communist areas. A strong, organic Atlantic Community could afford to seek some lessening of tension on its frontiers by giving general disarmament a local starting point—in the turning out of troops, in international inspection, in non-nuclear zones in such areas of collision as Central Europe, the Middle East, or Southeast Asia. So long as the Atlantic Alliance is an external association of unmerged national communities, its cohesion is always in doubt; even a change of ministry in one member-state may be enough to shatter its inner confidence. If nothing is really stable, no one can move for fear of starting the avalanche. We witness such immobility over Berlin. But an association created by a thousand unbreakable organic links—of trade, of development, of joint action, of common policies and purposes—is strong and resilient enough to show flexibility and compromise. If the Atlantic Alliance has no more solidity than a balloon, then a pinprick can be fatal to it. If it has the solidity of an organic world, surface modifications such as a demilitarization of the worst areas of tension will have no effect on its internal coherence.

At the same time a Western policy of controlled disarmaments, internal prosperity, and external generosity would modify in time the balance of political influence in the world. The Communists are losing the battle for influence in Western Europe because it offers to its millions of workers and peasants rising standards, better education, and the fact of freedom. The same battle can be lost by the Communists in the emergent lands provided the West's massive resources are used systematically to bring the underdeveloped "South" through the sound barrier of modernization. The old image of "capitalist exploiters" can be lost in the new image of free men setting their superabundant wealth to work to build up their neighbors' prosperity and independence. And who knows whether, among the newly educated millions of Russia itself, the fact of Western freedom, prosperity, and openhandedness may not ultimately make nonsense of the Marxist picture of "greedy imperialists" and tempt even the Communists into a policy of greater confidence and cooperation?

These perspectives may seem remote today. But there are times when free peoples have the duty to hope, to believe, as Sir Winston Churchill has put it, that "God has not despaired of His children." Communists may seem to us now to be implacable, intolerable enemies. But can we be certain whether, without their probing and challenging, we in the wealthy comfortable West would have ever become aware either of our own privilege or of others' needs? Would we have made the least progress towards a larger human solidity? Would we have had anything more than an inkling that the revolution of science and technology, by removing most limits on our material resources, adds a new and terrifying moral dimension to our freedom—the freedom to remedy or not the desperate poverty of millions of our fellow men? The hydrogen glare illumines an apocalyptic world. But it is apocalyptic in any case—in the physical unification of humanity, in the opportunities it offers for vision and generosity, in the inescapable obligation it lays on every Christian soul to use the new abundance for moral ends. Wrapped in wealth, bemused by our commercialized distractions, we might never have caught even a glimpse of this larger vision, had it not been for the insistent challenge pressed home, day in, day out, by World Communism. True, we can react to this challenge either with creative faith or fear. But it is inescapable, and the survival of mankind depends upon the quality of our response.

19TH- AND 20TH-CENTURY EUROPEAN HISTORY
TITLES IN THE NORTON LIBRARY

Aron, Raymond. *The Opium of the Intellectuals.* N106

Brandt, Conrad. *Stalin's Failure in China.* N352

Brinton, Crane. *The Lives of Talleyrand.* N188

Butterfield, Herbert. *The Whig Interpretation of History.* N318

Burn, W. L. *The Age of Equipoise.* N319

Eyck, Erich. *Bismarck and the German Empire.* N235

Ferrero, Guglielmo. *The Reconstruction of Europe.* N208

Feis, Herbert. *Europe: The World's Banker 1870-1914.* N327

Feis, Herbert. *The Spanish Story.* N339

Feis, Herbert. *Three International Episodes:* Seen from E. A. N351

Ford, Franklin L. *Strasbourg in Transition, 1648-1789.* N321

Graves, Robert and Alan Hodge. *The Long Week-end: A Social History of Great Britain, 1918-1939.* N217

Halperin, S. William. *Germany Tried Democracy.* N280

Hobsbawm, E. J. *Primitive Rebels.* N328

Langer, William L. *Our Vichy Gamble.* N379

Menéndez Pidal, Ramón. *The Spaniards in Their History.* N353

Pelling, Henry. *Modern Britain, 1885-1955.* N368

Rowse, A. L. *Appeasement.* N139

Russell, Bertrand. *Freedom versus Organization: 1814-1914.* N136

Whyte, A. J. *The Evolution of Modern Italy.* N298

Wolfers, Arnold. *Britain and France between Two Wars.* N343